Vegetable Cookery

Vegetable Cookery

by FLORENCE LaGANKE HARRIS

A. A. WYN, INC., NEW YORK

Foreword

THE NEXT time you go food shopping take time to look—really look—at the fresh-vegetable display. You scarcely can miss it. Extensive and brilliantly lighted, it has back walls of mirror glass which reflect fresh, colorful, perky vegetables. You may see some vegetables that look odd or unfamiliar, for modern methods of distribution have made foods national rather than regional. Okra has come North; avocados have come East; sweet corn has traveled to the West and the South. And vegetables are no longer seasonal: modern transportation brings all varieties to every section of the country the year round.

Other changes have taken place too; for example, in the housewares department, where open saucepans, kettles, and steamers used to be a major display. Now you find pressure saucepans and canners, casserole dishes of all sizes, and stream-lined chafing dishes. Cooking of vegetables has gone modern; the serving of them is now done with a flair.

Nutritional research has changed our concept of the contribution to health made by vegetables. We know now that the retention of maximum amounts of vitamins and minerals is in direct proportion to the proper cooking of vegetables; so is the pleasure we get from eating them.

The Vegetable Growers Association of America became increasingly aware of all these changes. Accordingly, they appointed a committee from the Women's Auxiliary of the Association. This committee was commissioned to look into the possibility of compiling a cookbook that would be in step with the changing times. The book was to contain recipes both old and new. It was to consider the whole field of fresh-vegetable buying and storing, cooking, and serving today's vegetables.

When this committee accepted the appointment, it may be said that this book began to take shape.

A cookbook is a combination handbook and reference book. The value of any reference book is directly related to its index, which should be full and complete. Great care has been taken with the index in this book. Cross indexing has been used to make it easy to find any recipe for any vegetable.

But a good index is more than a listing of the book's contents. It can, and should, be a source of inspiration and ideas. That, incidentally, is the theme and purpose of this book. Here are offered ways of using new vegetables, of making new combinations. The new techniques of cooking, canning, and freezing are stressed. All of which adds up to the author's hope that you, your family, and your guests will get new enjoyment from fresh vegetables!

FLORENCE LaGANKE HARRIS

Cleveland
February 1952

Acknowledgments

THE IDEA for this book was originated by the Vegetable Growers Association of America. Special acknowledgment is made to Marye Dahnke, Kraft Foods Company, Chicago; to Gladys Blair, J. Walter Thompson Company, Chicago, and to Mrs. John Fitkin, Sylvania, Ohio, who was President of the VGAA Ladies Auxiliary at the time the cookbook project was first discussed and adopted at the Indianapolis Convention in 1949.

Special appreciation goes to Mrs. Walter F. Pretzer for her assistance in planning the book and to Audrey B. Pretzer for help in compiling and organizing the material sent in by Auxiliary members.

Credit is due to the Cookbook Committee of the Women's Auxiliary of the Vegetable Growers Association of America: Mrs. Curtis Cook, Mrs. Sunny Christensen, Mrs. Clifton Cutting, and others. We wish to acknowledge with gratitude the contribution of a color frontispiece by the American Seed Trade Association.

FLORENCE LaGANKE HARRIS

Cleveland, Ohio
April, 1952

Contents

Vegetable Cookery

Handsome Is!

VICTORIAN mamas and grandmamas curbed the vanity of pretty misses by telling them that "Handsome is as handsome does, my dears."

Vegetables need no such advice, because handsome as they are, they always do handsomely by us, if given half a chance.

Walk through the dim green aisles of a hothouse where fresh vegetables are grown under glass; take an early morning stroll in your own vegetable garden; look at the display of fruits and vegetables at the greengrocer's, or at the supermarket, and you know—because your eyes have told you—that fresh vegetables are a handsome lot.

You see beauty in the varied shapes; you sense it in the fresh dewiness which old English writers called "verdure"; you are aware of it in the colors, which remind you of the palette of a painter.

[15]

Color runs through all its various shades and hues. See the pale ivory of summer squash and, at the other end of the yellow scale, the deep, rich orange of pumpkins and carrots.

Pale amethyst is found on a turnip's rounding top. Deep purple gives richness of color to eggplant.

Note the warm gray of mushrooms, the sandy tan of baking potatoes, the muted yellow of butternut squash, and the deep ocher of rutabagas. Admire the scarlet of tomatoes, the crimson of radishes, the tissue-paper whiteness of Bermuda onions.

And as for greens—that color ranges from the light green of kohlrabi, the buttery yellow-greens of curly endive hearts, the emerald and jade greens of leafy salad makings to the deep, deep green of peppers, cucumbers, and zucchini.

Truly a vegetable is handsome. Now, does it do handsomely by us?

Handsome Does

*Yes, Vegetables Can Do Handsomely
because of Their Composition*

BASIC SEVEN

THIS is why they tell us to eat vegetables: They contain nutrients we need.

Nutritionists the world over are in good agreement as to the amounts and kinds of nutrients a human being needs. The same nutrients (or substances that keep the body growing and in repair and working order) may be found in different foods in different countries.

North American food sources and food customs have crystallized our nutritionists' thinking into a list of seven basic food groups. Here is the list, with minimum daily servings:

[17]

GREEN AND YELLOW VEGETABLES
  1 large serving

ORANGES, TOMATOES, GRAPEFRUIT
  Or raw cabbage or raw greens
    1 serving

POTATOES AND OTHER VEGETABLES AND FRUITS
  1 or more potatoes
  2 servings of others

MILK AND MILK PRODUCTS
  As a beverage or in cooked foods
    Adults—1 pint
    Children—¾ to 1 quart
    Expectant and nursing mothers—1 quart

MEAT, POULTRY, FISH, EGGS
  1 serving meat, poultry, or fish
  1 egg (at least 4 a week)
  Dried beans, peas, nuts, or peanut butter

BREAD, FLOUR, CEREALS
  2 slices of bread or its equivalent at each meal
  Enriched or whole grain

BUTTER AND FORTIFIED MARGARINE
  With added vitamin A
  2 to 3 level tablespoons

  For growing children, additional vitamin D is important.

Note that vegetables star in three of the groups and are mentioned in a fourth one: meat, poultry, fish, and eggs, with dried beans and peas listed, as you can see. This particular group, incidentally, is the protein-rich group, and it is in the peas and beans or legumes that we find the greatest amount of protein in vegetables.

What are the nutrients and what do they do?

Proteins: Build and repair body tissue and assist in utilization of the other nutrients.

Carbohydrates (both starches and sugars): Furnish energy and aid in utilization of other nutrients.

Fats: Furnish energy and aid in utilization of other nutrients.

Water: Regulates body activities, keeps body from dehydration, assists in utilization of other nutrients.

Mineral Salts: Build bony and/or hard tissue, assist in utilization of other nutrients.

Vitamins (chemical compounds, usually found in certain foods, but sometimes formed within the human body from substances found in certain foods. These substances are called "provitamins"): Have varied functions, but are essential to life and growth; also assist in utilization of other nutrients. The number of vitamins is still unknown. Some, like vitamins A and D, are soluble in fat; others, the vitamins in vitamin B-complex and vitamin C, are soluble in water. (Exposure to air, light, heat, moisture cuts down effectiveness of most vitamins.)

Cellulose and hemi-celluloses are woody fibers found in most vegetables and fruits. They are not nutrients, but they are necessary since they furnish bulk and fiber, which assist in ridding the body of waste substances.

Percentage Composition of Vegetables

Taken by and large, 90 per cent, at least, of a vegetable is water. The remaining 10 per cent consists of varying amounts of celluloses or woody fibers, proteins, carbohydrates, fat, mineral salts, and vitamins.

Protein-rich: Peas, beans, lentils, soy beans. (These proteins are incomplete and need addition of animal proteins such as those in meat, fish, eggs, milk, cheese.)

Fat-rich: Avocado (17 per cent plus).

Starch-rich: Potatoes, sweet potatoes, corn (cooked).

Water-rich: Cucumber (96 per cent), lettuce, tomatoes, chicory, celery, asparagus, cabbage, corn (lowest in water content—78 per cent).

Mineral-rich:

Calcium: Leafy greens, bean family (including soy beans.)

Phosphorus: Legume family.

Iron: Peas, beans, lentils, leafy greens. Potatoes do not contain a large amount, but are listed as a valuable source, because of their frequency in our diet.

Vitamin-rich:

Vitamin A: Leafy, green, and yellow vegetables, tomatoes.

Vitamin B-complex: Thiamin—legumes (navy beans, lima beans, kidney beans, peas, lentils); riboflavin—green, leafy vegetables; niacin—green leafy vegetables, tomatoes.

Vitamin C: Raw cabbage, peppers, sweet potatoes, mustard greens, parsley, tomatoes either fresh or canned).

NOTE: When we say leafy green, green or yellow vegetables, we think of these:

Leafy green: Beet tops, broccoli, cabbage (green), chard, collards, dandelion greens, dock, escarole, kale, lamb's-quarters, lettuce (green leaf), mustard greens, parsley, purslane, spinach, turnip greens, watercress.

Green: Asparagus, beans (string), peas, peppers.

Yellow: Carrots, pumpkin, squash (yellow-fleshed, winter varieties), sweet potatoes.

Suppose a Vegetable Never Has a Chance

"Handsome is as handsome does,"—remember?—but sup-
pose a vegetable is never given a chance, what then?

What can happen to *raw* vegetables?

Much of a vegetable's food value is conditioned by the
kind of soil in which it has been grown, the sunshine it received, and the care given to storage. The mineral composition of a raw vegetable is affected by the soil in which the
vegetable is grown, but this is the problem of the truck
gardener and the grower of vegetables under glass, as well
as the home gardener. The vitamin content of a raw vegetable is affected by (1) the amount of sunshine to which the
vegetable is exposed during growth (this is especially true
of the part of the vegetable above the ground), (2) the maturity of the vegetable (vitamin content decreases once the peak
of maturity is past), and (3) the length of time elapsing between picking or harvesting of the vegetable and its appearance on the table (the decrease is rapid). The water content
of a raw vegetable may be decreased by the length of storage time, humidity, and the temperature of the atmosphere
surrounding the vegetable.

What is the best way to store vegetables to prevent their
drying out, molding, wilting, and general deterioration?

Root stock such as carrots, turnips, parsnips, and salsify
keep best in a cool spot where the moisture in the air is sufficient to prevent the withering or drying out of the vegetable.
These vegetables have a fairly heavy skin.

Leafy vegetables need cool, moist storage places.

Opinions differ regarding the storage of tomatoes. Some
growers feel that the flavor is impaired when the tomatoes
are kept in the refrigerator at any time.

Of all the vegetables known, sweet corn is the one that

should be cooked and eaten within a half hour after the ears have been taken from the parent stalk. No vegetable loses its desirable flavor quite so quickly after being picked as does sweet corn.

What can happen to *cooked* vegetables?

Cooks should be a vegetable's best friend, but they seldom are!

When is a vegetable properly cooked? When it retains the largest possible amount of the nutrients in it originally, when it still looks handsome, when it tastes fresh and "good," and when it still has a texture which is not mushy.

Why should vegetables be served promptly after being prepared? Standing around withers and shrinks a vegetable; reheating is likely to destroy flavor and color.

Leafy greens should be perky; root stock should not be soggy with water or steam; fresh green vegetables, like peas and beans, should not be mushy and shapeless. Reheating usually does that, especially if the vegetable was cooked way beyond the crunchy stage at the start.

Vitamins, minerals, color as well as texture are affected by cooking.

Vitamins: Vitamins are adversely affected by exposure to air, moisture, and heat. Some are water soluble. It becomes a question whether it is better to cut a potato, let's say, into fairly small pieces and thus lessen the cooking time, but increase the amount of cut surface exposed, or to leave the potato unpared and uncut with the necessary additional cooking time.

By and large, it is better to do no paring or peeling, no cutting previous to cooking. Since the greatest loss in vitamin value occurs in the time required to bring cooking water to boil plus the addition of the first two minutes of boiling time, it is best to put vegetables into water which is already boiling.

Minerals: Soaking of vegetables in water previous to cooking and boiling in large amounts of water tend to transfer soluble mineral salts from vegetable to water, therefore it is best not to soak vegetables, also best to gauge the cooking water so that little if any cooking liquid is left when the vegetable is cooked. If too much water is used, the liquid remaining when cooking is completed should be used in a sauce served with the vegetable, or drained and used later in vegetable drinks, or for the making of gravy, or soups.

Color: Steam in a covered saucepan or high temperature in a pressure cooker after a vegetable is cooked destroys the fresh color of green vegetables. So does reheating of these vegetables.

Cooking of Vegetables

fRESH, uncooked vegetables are pretty enough to "tempt a dying anchorite to eat." But an uncooked potato does not have taste appeal. A raw turnip is pungent, but the woody fiber is likely to upset human digestion.

Many vegetables are cooked to make them taste better and to make them easier for human digestive systems to manage.

But families grow tired of vegetables cooked simply and dressed with nothing but butter, salt, and pepper. For the sake of variety, many different recipes are given in this book. But DO remember that good foods simply cooked, like good dresses with simple lines, are considered smartest of all. Vegetables cooked simply and dressed with good butter, salt, and freshly ground pepper should be served often.

Nothing can be better than a freshly baked mealy potato. Take it from the oven as soon as it is soft, pop it open, and serve it at once with plenty of butter, and freshly ground salt and pepper. Chopped chives may be added.

Fresh green peas cooked in a minimum of boiling salted water, drained, and served with a dressing of butter or a little cream are superlatively good.

Ears of young, sweet corn cooked in boiling water and put on the table within a half hour from the time they were broken from the parent stalk need nothing but butter and salt to satisfy the most critical gourmet.

What is better than a tomato eaten out of hand just after being picked from the vine?

Remember: It's Smart to Serve Good Vegetables in the Simplest Form.

Basic Methods of Cooking Vegetables

NOTE: Frozen vegetables should be put into rapidly boiling water while the vegetable is still frozen hard as stone and bone. Do not defrost before cooking.

Top-range Cooking

Boiling—example, potatoes boiled in small amount of salted, boiling water.

Parboiling—example, beans partially cooked in boiling water.

Steaming—example, raw spinach placed in colander set above boiling water.

Braising—example, raw vegetable, small amount of butter or margarine, blanketed in lettuce leaf.

Pressure cooking—example, green peas (fresh or frozen) cooked in small amount of superheated steam.

Pan-frying—example, slices of eggplant cooked on griddle or in frying pan in small amount of melted fat.

Deep-fat frying—example, rings of raw onions sprinkled with

seasoned flour or dipped in batter before being dropped
into the hot fat.

OVEN COOKING

Baking in dry heat—example, baked potatoes, acorn squash.
Escalloping—example, baking a prepared vegetable in moisture of its own (tomatoes), or with moisture added, (potatoes). Escalloping is done in an uncovered casserole or
baking dish.
Braising—example, baking a vegetable with little, if any,
added moisture (braised celery in covered baking dish).
Oven frying—example, Potatoes Anna (raw potato slices
dipped in melted fat and baked on a shallow pan).
Souffléing—example, a vegetable purée, heavy cream sauce,
with stiffly beaten whites of eggs folded in, baked in a
heavy dish.

BROILER COOKING

Broiling under direct heat—example, broiled tomato slices.

Timetable for Covered Saucepan Cooking of Vegetables

*Cooking time is computed from the time when the water gets
back to the boiling point after the vegetables have been added.*

Artichokes
    French or globe .... 20-30 mins.
    Jerusalem, whole .... 30-45 mins.
Asparagus .... 10-20 mins.
Beans, shell or string .... 15-20 mins.
Beet greens .... 8-12 mins.
Beets, young .... 20-45 mins.
    old .... 2-4 hrs.
Broccoli .... 12-15 mins.

Brussels sprouts .... 15-20 mins.
Cabbage .... 8-12 mins.
Carrots, young whole .... 15-20 mins.
        old .... 20-30 mins.
Cauliflower, whole .... 15-25 mins.
Celery .... 10-20 mins.
Corn .... 7-12 mins.
Cucumber .... 10-15 mins.
Dandelion greens .... 8-12 mins.
Eggplant, sautéed .... 6-10 mins.
Kohlrabi, whole .... 18-25 mins.
Leeks .... 10-15 mins.
Okra .... 15-25 mins.
Onions .... 15-45 mins.
Parsnips .... 25-35 mins.
Peas, green .... 12-15 mins.
Potatoes, white .... 20-45 mins.
        sweet .... 25-30 mins.
Salsify .... 18-25 mins.
Spinach .... 8-12 mins.
Squash, summer .... 12-20 mins.
      winter, steamed .... 45-60 mins.
Tomatoes .... 10-12 mins.
Turnips, diced small .... 12-20 mins.

Pressure Cooking of Vegetables

Pressure cookers are of two shapes, a large-pressure canner and a smaller, saucepan-shaped cooker called, more properly, a pressure saucepan.

Each manufacturer has his own patented device for measuring and maintaining desired pressures. Follow the directions which come with your make of saucepan.

Never fill saucepan more than ⅔ full of uncooked food and water.

The minimum amount of water is ¼ cup. This is used for small and green vegetables. The maximum amount is ¾ cup. This amount (or possibly ½ cup) is used for solid vegetables, such as beets, kohlrabi, potatoes, whole onions, pumpkins.

The amount of water called for in the following table is not increased as the amount of vegetable to be cooked is increased. One cup or one quart of a given vegetable will require the same amount of water.

What are the advantages of pressure cooking? The brief cooking time, the small amount of liquid, and the high temperature tend to keep color fresh, soften fibers, keep the loss of vitamins and minerals at a minimum, and retain the flavor at its best.

All of these advantages are lost, however, if the vegetables are overcooked, or allowed to stand in the cooker while the pressure slowly falls. Reduce the pressure as soon as the cooking time is finished. Hold the cooker (cover still on, of course) under running cold water until the pressure is down to zero.

Remember that a pressure cooker—time- and flavor-saver that it is—cannot work miracles. No better-quality vegetable can come out of it than goes in.

Timetable for Pressure Saucepan Cooking of Fresh Vegetables

Vegetable	Cups water	Pounds cooking pressure	Minutes cooking time
Artichoke	1	15	15
Asparagus	¼	15	1½
Beans: Lima	⅓	5	2
Beans: snap	¼	15	4

Timetable for Pressure Saucepan Cooking of Fresh Vegetables (continued)

Vegetable	Cups water	Pounds cooking pressure	Minutes cooking time
Beets:			
large whole	¾	15	18
small whole	¾	15	12
slices	½	15	6
Broccoli	¼	15	2-3
Brussels sprouts	¼	15	3
Cabbage:			
shredded	½	15	3
2-3 inch wedges	¾	15	4-6
red	½	15	5
Carrots:			
sliced	¼	15	3
whole	¼	15	4-8
Cauliflower:			
whole	½	15	6-8
flowerets	½	15	3
Celeriac	¼	15	5
Celery	¼	15	5
Corn-on-cob	¼	15	3
Kale	¼	15	4
Kohlrabi	½	15	4
Okra	¼	15	3
Onions:			
sliced	¼	15	3
whole	½	15	10
Parsnips:			
halves	½	15	7
sliced	½	15	2

Timetable for Pressure Saucepan Cooking of Fresh Vegetables (continued)

Vegetable	Cups water	Pounds cooking pressure	Minutes cooking time
Peas	¼	5	2
Potatoes:			
medium whole	½	15	15
cut-up	½	15	8
Potatoes, sweet:			
whole	½	15	6
quartered	½	15	6
Pumpkin	¾	15	8
Rutabagas: cut up	¼	15	5
Spinach and other greens	¼	15	1½
Squash:			
acorn	¾	15	5
butternut	¼	15	10
hubbard	¾	15	10-12
summer	½	15	8-10
Tomatoes: whole	½	15	5
Turnips	½	15	5
Zucchini	¼	15	2

Aids to Flavor

HERBS

To the uninitiated, an herb garden looks like a plot of weeds. That's easy to understand, because the leaves are small and the blossoms are most inconspicuous. But what herbs lack in showiness they make up in the magic of their scent and flavor.

Monosodium Glutamate

Monosodium glutamate, a protein derived from grains, is sold in powdered form under brand names such as ACCENT, ZEST, MSG. It brings out the flavor of vegetables.

Modified French Cooking Method for Vegetables

Butter or margarine, well-washed vegetables, lettuce-leaf blanket, low heat, and a tightly covered saucepan are needed to cook vegetables in the French provincial way.

Select a heavy saucepan. Melt 1 tablespoon butter or margarine for each serving of vegetable (servings for 4 require ⅛ pound). Add the raw vegetable prepared for cooking as usual. Add about ½ teaspoon sugar and ½ teaspoon salt.

Cover the vegetables in the saucepan with a washed, but not drained, lettuce leaf.

Cook over LOW heat. This is important, because the lack of water leads to quick scorching.

Cooking time is just about the same as that for vegetables cooked in boiling water in the usual way.

The French method gives vegetables an excellent flavor. Their appearance is attractive, too.

Measurements

All measurements are level

3 teaspoons equal 1 tablespoon

16 tablespoons equal 1 cup

Standard measuring cup holds $\frac{1}{2}$ pint

Artichokes, French or Globe and Jerusalem

Theophilus Thistle, that sifter of thistles—
While prickles on thistles grew thicker than bristles—
Was writing a treatise on thistles and thieves
And wishing that thistles had nothing but leaves.

THEOPHILUS should be getting acquainted with globe artichokes if he wants to find thistles with little but leaves. True,
the globe artichoke does have a small choke, or prickly thistle
section, down in the fleshy heart. But surrounding this base
and giving the vegetable its descriptive name are green leaves
shaped and curved to make something that looks like a globe.

BUYING GUIDE: Compact, heavy globes; with large, curved,
tightly clinging, fleshy leaf scales; dark green color indicates

freshness; size has little to do with quality or flavor. Loose, spreading, discolored leaves indicate overmaturity and poor quality.

Jerusalem artichokes are underground tubers. They are rather knobby in shape. The skin is thin, speckled tan in color.

The method of cooking is given in Creamed Jerusalem Artichokes (page 40).

Basic Rule for Cooking Globe Artichokes

Wash artichoke in running water. Make a straight crosscut about 1 inch below leafy tips. Discard these ends.

Tie string around middle of each globe to keep the globe in a compact bundle during cooking.

Cook in rapidly boiling salted water. When sharp fork tine pierces fleshy base easily the vegetable is cooked.

Remove from hot water, invert, and drain.

Cooked artichokes may be served HOT as a vegetable or COLD as a salad.

HOT ARTICHOKES

Place one hot artichoke on small plate. Beside it place a small dish containing melted butter, with or without lemon juice, or hot Hollandaise sauce.

Only the pulpy flesh at the base of each leaf and the pulpy center, or heart, are eaten. Pull off a leaf; dip its fleshy base in sauce.

Insert base of leaf between lips. Close teeth upon it. Gently draw leaf away from mouth, leaving pulp in mouth. Discard leaf.

When eating pulpy base or heart, discard spiny "choke" at center of heart.

GLOBE ARTICHOKE RING WITH ASPARAGUS TIPS

2 cups artichoke bottoms   ½ teaspoon salt
2 tablespoons butter   4 eggs
2 tablespoons flour   1 cup fine cracker crumbs
½ cup cream   Cooked asparagus tips

Cook and mash artichoke bottoms (see page 38). Make a thick white sauce with butter, flour, and cream (see page 219). Remove from heat and add salt. Beat egg yolks until light. When white sauce is slightly cooled, stir in egg yolks. Add cracker crumbs. Fold in mashed artichokes.

Beat egg whites until stiff and fold into above mixture. Pour into a buttered ring mold. Set in pan of warm water and bake at 350 degrees, for about 45 minutes, or until set. Remove ring from oven and let stand for a few minutes.

Turn onto a hot platter and fill center with buttered or creamed asparagus tips.

Serves 6.

CREAMED JERUSALEM ARTICHOKES

3 pounds artichokes   2 cups milk
2 cups water   1 teaspoon lemon juice
1 tablespoon vinegar   ¼ teaspoon salt
½ teaspoon salt   ¼ teaspoon sugar
3 tablespoons butter   1/16 teaspoon pepper
4 tablespoons flour   2 egg yolks
            2 tablespoons heavy cream

Scrape artichokes and cut into one-inch cubes. Cook until tender in boiling water, vinegar, and salt, about 15 to 20 minutes.

Melt butter, add flour, and heat thoroughly before adding the milk, stirring briskly to avoid lumps. Season and simmer 4 to 5 minutes. You may enrich the sauce by adding egg yolks. In that case, stir the yolks well and blend with cream. Pour a little of the hot sauce over this mixture. Then pour it back into the kettle to simmer 4 to 5 minutes, without boiling.

Fold in the artichokes gently. Sprinkle the top with chopped parsley.

Serves 6.

*   *   *

Additional recipes for artichokes will be found under Pickles and Relishes, Salads, and Home Canning of Vegetables.

Asparagus

I︎T COMES as something of a shock to read that as far back as 1678 John Evelyn Esquire advocated quick and short cooking of asparagus (and we think short-time cookery is a recent discovery). In his discourse on "Sallets" he writes:

Sparagus, easy of digestion; may be eaten raw except for a bitterness which is drawn out in cooking; being so speedily boiled as not to lose the verdure and agreeable tenderness; which is done by letting the water boil before you put them in. We, in England, prejudice both sparagus and coleworts by overboiling them, thereby their volatile salts (in which much of their virtue consists) are evaporated. The Romans did with that celerity boil their sparagus that Augustus, when he ordered any business to be expedited, his proverbial saying was "Let it be dispatch'd 'citius quam asparagi coquuntur.' "

BUYING GUIDE: Two types, white and green. Green more desirable. Should be green almost entire length of stalk. Tender brittle stalks with compact tips. White asparagus milder in flavor than green, should be white entire length of stalk except for tip, other characteristics same as green. Beware of angular stalks.

Basic Rule for Cooking Fresh Asparagus

Fresh asparagus used to herald the coming of spring. Now it is available early and late. But the first asparagus of the season, served hot and dressed with butter, or a little rich cream, is still exciting. The flavor is so good, like that of no other vegetable.

Clean asparagus gently, but thoroughly. Grains of sand hide under the petals or scales at the blossom end. To remove the sand, you may have to scrape off these scales. Do this under running water.

The stalk may be woody at its base. Make tentative cuts along the stalk with a sharp knife. When your knife penetrates the stalk easily you know the stalk is edible from that point on. Cut off and discard the woody part.

Stalks may be cut into 2-inch lengths or left intact. If cut into short pieces, set the blossom ends aside temporarily, because they cook in a shorter time than the rest of stalk.

ASPARAGUS WITH BUTTER OR CREAM

To cook cut-up stalks: Put all but heads into rapidly boiling salted water. When pieces are almost tender, add the heads. Do not overcook. Serve with butter or cream.

To cook whole stalks: Tie five or six stalks into a bundle. Stand these bundles in a deep saucepan holding rapidly boiling, salted water. The rising steam cooks the tender heads while the swirling water cooks the stalk. A special asparagus cooker may be used; this is a tall, slender double-boiler affair with perforated bottom and sides in upper part. The perforations allow the boiling water in the lower part to come in contact with the stalks, while the rising steam cooks the tender heads.

Five or six whole stalks are a portion. Melted butter to which a little lemon juice and crunchy toasted bread crumbs have been added may be spooned over the stalks at serving time.

ASPARAGUS PUDDING

2 cups asparagus	½ teaspoon salt
3 eggs	1/16 teaspoon cayenne
2 cups milk	1/16 teaspoon nutmeg
2 tablespoons melted butter	

Cut asparagus in 1-inch pieces. Cook until tender.

Beat eggs slightly. Add milk and season. Add asparagus and melted butter.

Pour this mixture into baking dish.

Place in water bath and bake at 350 degrees 40 to 50 minutes, or until custard is completely set. Test by inserting silver-knife blade. If blade comes out clean, the custard is done.

This dish, like its cousin—corn pudding—is an excellent vegetable dish to serve with broiled or pan-fried chops. Try it with loin lamb chops.

Serves 6.

HAM AND ASPARAGUS ROLLS

24 stalks asparagus
6 thin slices ham
Simple Cheese Sauce (page 226)

Cook asparagus until just tender.
Broil ham on both sides.

On each slice of ham place several stalks of asparagus. Roll up like a jelly roll.

Serve with a generous amount of the cheese sauce poured over each of the ham rolls.

Serves 6.

*   *   *

Additional recipes for asparagus will be found under Salads, Soups, How To Freeze Vegetables, and Home Canning of Vegetables.

Avocados

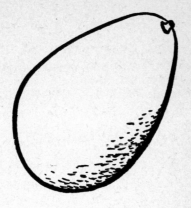

Botanically speaking, an avocado is the fruit of the plant. It is usually displayed, however, in the vegetable section of a shop. Other names for it are *aguacate,* alligator pear, and Calavo. The last name designates such avocados as are grown in California.

The place of origin of the avocado is South America.

The soft green-colored pulp is buttery in texture and rich in fat. The sharp fruity acid of grapefruit or the tartness of French dressing is needed to make this vegetable palatable. However, it may be mashed and seasoned and used as a spread, or as a dip for potato chips. Avocado may also be used as an ingredient of ice cream.

Buying Guide: Avocados vary greatly in color, size, and appearance; color varies from green to almost black; size ranges from 5 ounces to 3 pounds. Avocados vary from spherical to pear shape; skin may be thick, thin, rough, or smooth.

Ripeness is indicated by bright fresh appearance and fairly firm flesh; brown scabs on skin are superficial, do not affect quality of flesh. Avoid avocados with dark, soft, sunken spots on surface, or punctured skin.

Basic Rule for Avocados

Avocados are buttery in texture, rich and bland in flavor. The flesh turns dark almost immediately upon exposure to air. Lemon juice, tart French dressing, or grapefruit juice spooned over the cut surface prevents rapid darkening. And any one of these dressings is an excellent foil for the richness of avocado salad.

Wash avocado. Cut into halves lengthwise. Give halves a slight twist to separate them. Remove large seed and discard it. Pull off, rather than pare, the skin. It comes off much like a glove. The peeled halves may be left intact or sliced for salads.

Thin slices may be floated on clear soups.

Avocado may be added to creamed turkey or chicken. Cut raw avocado into cubes and add to creamed mixture about 5 minutes before serving.

BAKED AVOCADO WITH ASPARAGUS

2 avocados	1/3 cup sliced pimiento *or*
1½ cups medium white sauce (page 219)	1 tablespoon chopped green pepper *or*
1½ cups diced cooked asparagus	2 tablespoons chopped parsley
	4 slices bacon

Cut avocados into halves lengthwise. Remove seed, but leave skin on half shells.

Sprinkle lightly with salt. Fill with heated mixture of white sauce and vegetables. Top with bacon slices cut into halves.

Place filled shells in shallow baking pan. Cover bottom of pan with warm water.

Set pan in 350-degree preheated oven. Bake for 5 minutes. Serve at once.

Almost any creamed combination may be put into the half shells. In place of bacon strips freshly crumbed bread lightly toasted or grated cheese may be used.

Serves 6.

*   *   *

Additional recipes for avocado will be found under Appetizers, Salads, and Soups.

Beans, Snap and Lima

THE BEAN family is large and diversified.

Pole and bush beans are two contrasting beanplant growths.

Snap beans are beans in pods which snap when doubled between thumb and fingers; many varieties are on sale. *String* used to be the descriptive term, but present-day snap beans no longer have a tough fiber or string to zip the pods shut. Green is sometimes applied to green podded beans to distinguish them from yellow—wax or butter—beans.

Lima beans are always shelled before cooking, whereas snap beans are not. The pod of the Lima bean is tough, large, and flat enough to house individual beans which are likewise quite flat, and kidney-shaped.

Lima beans retain freshness longer if not shelled until just before cooking.

Soy beans have never been accepted in the United States

as enthusiastically as they are in China. Most Americans still think of soy beans as a cover-plant used to put nitrogen back in the soil.

BUYING GUIDE: Snap beans should be firm, crisp, plump, bright-colored. Lima beans should have well-filled pods, a deep green color, should be clean and fresh. No bean pod should be ridgy or overly bulged, nor should it be flabby, leathery, or yellowed (signs of overmaturity). Decay is shown by a watery condition, or mold.

Basic Rule for Cooking Snap Beans

Snap beans, either green or yellow, are certainly the gardener's friend! One short row of bean plants in the home garden produces beans and beans and BEANS!

Good as beans are in themselves, their flavor is improved, many cooks believe, if a small amount of summer savory (bohnenkraut) is cooked with them.

Wash beans. Cut or break off the blossom tip and stem end.

Beans may be left whole, cut into inch lengths, or Frenched: that is, cut into long slender ribbons. These lengths may be cut on the "bias" if desired.

Nutritionally speaking, cooked beans contain the greatest amount of minerals and vitamins when the bean is left uncut. A word to the wise . . .

Drop prepared beans into a small amount of rapidly boiling salted water. Cooking time should be short; otherwise, bean is mushy and dingy green in color.

Try varying the appearance and flavor of green or wax beans. For instance:

BUTTERED BEANS

Dress cooked beans with small amount of butter.

BEANS WITH CREAM

Dress cooked beans with a small amount of cream.

CREAMED BEANS

Dress cooked beans with a thin cream or white sauce (page 219).

BEANS WITH CHESTNUTS

Combine cooked beans with halved cooked chestnuts. Add butter.

BEANS WITH SALTED ALMONDS

Add coarsely chopped salted almonds to buttered green beans. Do this just before serving.

BEANS WITH SAUTÉED MUSHROOMS

Add sautéed mushroom caps to buttered beans.

BEANS WITH CARROTS

Vary the familiar peas-and-carrot mixture by adding sliced cooked carrots to cooked beans cut into inch lengths. Season with a suspicion of nutmeg.

Basic Rule for Cooking Lima Beans

Shell the beans, discarding the pod. Cook in a small amount of boiling salted water until beans are tender when pierced with a fork.

BUTTERED LIMA BEANS

Dress cooked beans with small amount of butter.

CREAMED LIMA BEANS

Dress cooked beans with cream, or a thin cream sauce.

HERBED LIMA BEANS

Add 5 or 6 fresh leaves of summer savory or ⅛ teaspoon of crumbled dried leaves of the herb during the cooking of the beans.

BEANS AND TOMATOES

5 slices bacon	2 cups tomatoes, cooked
2 onions, sliced	1 teaspoon salt
½ pound green beans	Pepper
	Monosodium glutamate

Dice bacon. Cook in frying pan until pieces are crisp. Add onion and sauté lightly.

Add Frenched green beans (page 49), tomatoes, and seasonings. Cover. Cook until beans are tender.

Serves 6.

GREEN BEANS WITH SOUR CREAM

4 cups green beans
Salt and pepper
½ cup sour cream

Prepare green beans in usual manner (page 49). Drain excess liquid. Add salt, pepper, and sour cream.

Serves 6.

SWEET-SOUR WAX BEANS

4 cups wax beans	Seasonings
¼ cup vinegar	½ cup water
	¼ cup brown sugar

Cut beans in 1-inch pieces. Cook in boiling salted water. Drain.

Make sirup of remaining ingredients. Pour over hot beans. Bring to a boil. Serve hot.

Serves 6.

CASSEROLE OF LIMAS

2½ cups cooked Lima beans	2 cups tomato purée
1 large onion, chopped	Salt and pepper
1 green pepper, chopped	Worcestershire sauce
1 small clove garlic	Monosodium glutamate
2 tablespoons fat	1½ cups grated cheese

Sauté chopped pepper, onion, and garlic in fat. Add tomato purée and simmer for 20 minutes.

Add Lima beans. Season. Simmer for 15 minutes more.

Make layers of beans and cheese, ending with cheese on top, in baking dish.

Bake at 350 degrees about 20 minutes, or until top browns and mixture bubbles.

Serves 6.

*   *   *

Additional recipes for beans will be found under Pickles and Relishes, Salads, Soups, How To Freeze Vegetables, and Home Canning of Vegetables.

Beets

"BLESSED be the person who first concocted the dish called 'Harvard beets' " say cooks when they are looking for a red food.

Beets are root-stock vegetables possessing solidity and varying amounts of woody fiber. The nutritional contribution is largely carbohydrate.

Beet sugar is made from a different variety of beets than the one used for food. Beet sugar, incidentally, has the same chemical formula as cane sugar and may be used successfully in any recipe calling for sugar.

BUYING GUIDE: Beets should have a good globular shape; be hard, clean, bright red, uniform in size; have smooth, firm flesh. Rough beets with growth cracks may be tough and woody; flabby or shriveled beets lack flavor. Select beets without numerous leaf scars around tops.

Beet tops, or beet greens should be clean, fresh, tender, young, and thin-ribbed. Avoid wilted, slimy tops.

NOTE: Wilted or damaged beet tops do not affect the quality of the root.

Basic Rule for Cooking Beets

If tops are on beets, remove leafy part, cutting off about 1 inch from beet globe or bulb. Small tap roots may be pulled off. Wash well. Thorough washing is necessary since beets are usually cooked with the skins left on.

Washed beets may be put into a heavy, tightly covered casserole and baked until tender in a 300-degree oven.

They may be cooked in a large amount of rapidly boiling salted water.

Cooking time is shortened if beets are cooked in a pressure saucepan. In this case they may be pared and cubed, if desired.

When beets are tender (insert sharp tined fork), they are peeled easily. Hold a beet under running cold water. Work skin off, using gentle pressure of fingers.

BUTTERED BEETS

Skinned cooked beets may be left whole, diced, or sliced and dressed with melted butter.

SPICY BEETS

Skinned cooked beets may be dressed with a little vinegar and melted butter. The vinegar may be wine vinegar or tarragon vinegar.

The vinegar may be "mulled": simmered for a short time with a piece of stick cinnamon, a small amount of feathery dill, a suspicion of sugar, and a whole clove or two. Strain vinegar before adding butter and pouring over the hot beets.

BEETS PIQUANT

12 beets
3 tablespoons melted butter
2 tablespoons vinegar or
  sherry

½ teaspoon salt
1 teaspoon sugar
1 teaspoon prepared mustard
  (optional)

Parsley

Cook and peel the beets. Combine butter and seasonings
and bring just to a boil. Pour sauce over the beets.
Garnish with parsley.

Serves 4.

STUFFED BEETS

8 to 10 beets, cooked
2 cups water
¼ teaspoon salt
¼ cup rice, raw
½ cup blanched almonds,
  chopped

4 tablespoons butter or
  margarine
Seasonings to taste
2 tablespoons chopped chives

Scoop out beets, leaving walls about ¼ inch thick. Flatten
bottom surfaces so beets stand firm.

Cook rice in boiling salted water. When rice is tender,
drain. Add remaining ingredients.

Stuff beets with mixture. Place beets in shallow baking
dish. Bake them for 20 minutes in a 350-degree oven.

Serves 4 to 5.

CALICO DUMPLINGS

2 cups sifted flour
3 teaspoons baking powder
  (double-acting)

1 teaspoon salt
2 tablespoons shortening
¾ cup milk

1 cup cooked beets, chopped

Sift together dry ingredients. Cut in shortening. Add milk and beets quickly to dry mixture. Stir lightly just until combined.

Drop by spoonfuls into boiling broth. Cover tightly and cook 15 minutes.

Serves 6.

HARVARD BEETS

10 to 12 small beets, cooked   ¼ cup vinegar
1/3 cup sugar   ¼ cup cooking liquid or water
2 teaspoons cornstarch   1 tablespoon butter
                    Salt to taste

Cook beets. Remove skin. Leave beets whole or cut in cubes or slices. Set aside temporarily.

Mix sugar and cornstarch. Add vinegar and cooking liquid or water and boil 5 minutes. Add beets and let stand over hot water ½ hour. Heat thoroughly and add butter before serving.

Serves 6.

RED FLANNEL HASH

4 cups chopped cooked potato   ½ cup cream
1½ cups chopped cooked beets   Salt, pepper, monosodium
½ onion, chopped   glutamate, celery salt, to
1 cup chopped cooked corned   taste
  beef   1 tablespoon margarine

Chop each vegetable separately. Chop meat. Do not put all ingredients in chopping bowl at one time. After chopping, mix ingredients lightly. Season and moisten mixture with cream.

Melt margarine in heavy frying pan. Spread mixture in

pan. Brown slowly over low fire. At serving time, fold one half over other, bringing crusty bottom on top.

Serves 6.

*   *   *

Additional recipes for beets will be found under Appetizers, Pickles and Relishes, Salads, Soups, How To Freeze Vegetables, and Home Canning of Vegetables.

*   *   *

BEET GREENS *(see* Greens, page 99).

Broccoli

ITALIANS use this branch of the cabbage family much more widely than do Americans. In this country, broccoli is considered a slightly more dressy green vegetable than beans, spinach, or even peas. Accordingly, it is found chiefly on menus for company or special dinners.

BUYING GUIDE: Green stalks with tight compact buds. Buds should be dark green or purplish green; avoid those with a yellow- or purple-colored bloom. Size of heads bears no relation to eating quality. Wilted, flabby, or woody product is unsatisfactory.

Basic Rule for Cooking Broccoli

Looking for a rich color to accent a rather pale meat and vegetable course? The answer is deep green broccoli, served with Hollandaise sauce.

[58]

Looking for a chance to establish your reputation as an intelligent vegetable cook? The answer lies in the cooked broccoli you serve. It is shapely; tender but not mushy; has been given richness with melted butter and zest with lemon juice, wine, or tarragon vinegar.

Broccoli heads or blossoms with only short lengths of tender stalk are the parts cooked and served.

Wash broccoli thoroughly, but gently, in running warm water. Look blossoms over carefully to detect tiny, almost invisible insect infestation (not all broccoli is infested).

Discard the stalk below the point where a sharp knife blade cuts into it easily.

Broccoli blossoms or heads, like those of asparagus, are tender and cook quickly. Use small amount of rapidly boiling salted water; or cook, with care, in pressure saucepan (reduce steam pressure quickly if pressure method is used). Drain. Serve while very hot.

BUTTERED BROCCOLI

Dress hot cooked broccoli with melted butter.

BROCCOLI WITH BUTTER AND VINEGAR

Dress hot cooked broccoli with melted butter to which a small amount of vinegar has been added. Herbal vinegars may be used. Lemon juice may be substituted for vinegar.

BROCCOLI WITH HOLLANDAISE SAUCE

Place hot cooked broccoli on individual serving dishes. Spoon a generous amount of Hollandaise sauce on vegetable, leaving blossom part uncovered.

BROCCOLI WITH POPPY SEED

1 pound broccoli	Juice of ½ lemon
1 cup water	1 teaspoon poppy seed
Salt	¼ teaspoon paprika
¼ cup butter	1/16 teaspoon cayenne

Wash broccoli thoroughly. Discard tough ends of stalks.

Cook broccoli in salted water until heads are tender but not mushy. Drain.

Melt butter, add remaining ingredients, and pour over hot broccoli.

Serves 4.

CHICKEN DIVAN

8 branches broccoli, cooked
8 large slices cooked chicken
  (white meat)

3 cups Sauce Mornay
1 cup American cheese, grated
¼ teaspoon paprika

Drain cooked broccoli and arrange in bottom of shallow casserole. Cover with slices of chicken and completely cover with Sauce Mornay. Sprinkle with cheese and paprika.

Bake in 350-degree oven until brown (approximately 4 minutes).

Turkey may be substituted for chicken.

Sauce Mornay

1 cup thick cream sauce
  (page 220)
1 cup heavy cream

1 cup American cheese
⅛ teaspoon cayenne pepper
Salt and pepper

Place cream sauce and heavy cream in small saucepan. Mix well. Bring to a gentle boil. Add cheese and cayenne pepper. Allow to simmer until cheese is melted and the sauce has a smooth appearance. Add salt and pepper to taste.

Serves 4 to 6.

*   *   *

Additional recipes for broccoli will be found under Soups and How To Freeze Vegetables.

Brussels Sprouts

Having a dinner guest whose hobby is collecting miniatures?
Then Brussels sprouts are what you should serve. These tiny
heads sprout along a main stalk or stem rather than heading
close to the ground like their relative the cabbage. The tiny
heads are detached from the stalk when picked for marketing.

Sprouts received their name from the spot where they grow
luxuriously, just outside the city of Brussels in Belgium.

Buying Guide: Hard, round, compact; bright-green coloring. Smudgy, dirty appearance may indicate presence of insects. Yellow leaves or puffiness in the Brussels sprout indicates age and staleness.

Basic Rule for Cooking Brussels Sprouts

Brussels sprouts enjoy a reputation and appreciation way
and beyond their diminutive size. And well they may. Cooked

[61]

briefly in boiling salted water they retain a fresh color, a mild flavor, and a gentle crunchiness.

Wash them gently. Look carefully for small holes, which indicate presence of insects. After removing wilted outer leaves, cut around any such holes.

Cook sprouts in small amount of rapidly boiling salted water. Watch timing carefully if using a pressure saucepan.

When served they should be hot and a beautiful fresh green.

BUTTERED BRUSSELS SPROUTS

Serve hot, dressed with melted butter.

BRUSSELS SPROUTS WITH VINEGAR

Dress cooked hot sprouts with plain or herbal vinegar and melted butter. Do not use much vinegar.

BRUSSELS SPROUTS WITH ALMONDS

Add coarsely chopped salted almonds with melted butter just before serving.

BRUSSELS SPROUTS WITH CHESTNUTS

Cut boiled chestnuts into halves or large pieces. Sprinkle over sprouts. Add melted butter.

*   *   *

Additional recipes for Brussels sprouts will be found under Home Canning of Vegetables.

Cabbage

More than alliteration may have caused Lewis Carroll to couple "cabbages and kings." The Greeks held cabbage in such high respect that they swore by it as being something high and holy, even as were kings in days gone by.

The cabbage family is large. Included are broccoli, collards, Brussels sprouts, cauliflower, kale (borecole), kohlrabi, red cabbage, and curly cabbage as well as the well-known green cabbage.

If cauliflower, ivory-white-headed, is the cabbage that went to college, then members of the cabbage family that never developed a head, like kale and collards, must be the ignoramuses of the family. Head cabbage, the kind most used, must represent the good businessmen of the family—hardheaded and not too concerned with frills or beauty.

BUYING GUIDE: Domestic cabbage is green, with a somewhat

loose-leaved flat head. *Danish* cabbage is green, tight-leaved, with a roundish head. *Savoy* cabbage has yellowish crimped leaves forming a rather loose head. Red cabbage, deep or purplish red, is a round and solid head. Heads should be well-trimmed, firm, leafy, for their size. Avoid coarse, discolored veins. If outer-base leaves are detached from main stem, cabbage will be strong-flavored and coarse-textured. Soft or puffy heads are poor in quality.

Basic Rule for Cooking Cabbage

Overcooking cabbage is so easy that it is not surprising it is so common. But it's unfortunate, to say the least. The limp, soggy, dingy mess called "boiled cabbage" must be a blow to the cabbage's pride.

Wash cabbage. Remove any wilted outer leaves. Look for traces of worm infestation (seldom seen in commercially grown cabbage).

Cut head in halves or quarters. Cut out and discard pieces of central core.

The quarters or eighths may be cooked as is in boiling salted water, or may be given a brief cooking in the water in which a piece of corned beef is simmering. But ordinarily, the sections are loosely shredded or sliced before being plunged into boiling water.

Cooking may take as little as 8 minutes, with 12 minutes the maximum.

Drain and serve hot.

BUTTERED CABBAGE

Dress hot cabbage with melted butter.

BUTTERED CABBAGE WITH CARAWAY SEEDS

Dress hot cabbage with butter and sprinkle caraway seeds over it.

BUTTERED CABBAGE WITH BUTTER AND VINEGAR

Dress cabbage with melted butter. Add a small amount of vinegar (cider, wine, or herbal).

CABBAGE WITH CREAM

Add a small amount of cream to hot cooked cabbage.

FRIED CABBAGE

4 tablespoons margarine
6 cups finely chopped cabbage
½ teaspoon salt
2 tablespoons brown sugar
¼ teaspoon dry mustard
½ cup sour cream
3 tablespoons vinegar

Sauté cabbage in margarine for 15 minutes; stir frequently.
Add other ingredients. Heat to boiling point.
Serve hot.
Serves 6.

RED CABBAGE AND APPLES WITH WINE

1 head red cabbage
3 apples
3 tablespoons butter
¼ cup vinegar
½ tablespoon flour
½ cup brown sugar
1 teaspoon salt
Black pepper, freshly ground
½ cup California red wine

Cut cabbage fine. Cook until tender, about 10 minutes, using small amount of water. Drain.
Peel apples, slice, and cook in water until tender.
Brown butter. Add cabbage and apples.
Add vinegar, flour, sugar, salt, pepper. Add wine last.
Cook about 10 minutes.
Serves 6.

ESCALLOPED CABBAGE

4 cups cabbage, shredded	1 cup cabbage liquid
3 tablespoons margarine	½ cup Cheddar cheese
3 tablespoons flour	Seasonings
1 cup top milk	Crumbled potato chips

Cook cabbage in boiling salted water for 12 minutes. Drain. Reserve 1 cup cooking liquid.

Melt margarine. Add flour. Cook until mixture is bubbling. Add combined milk and cabbage liquid. Bring to boil. Add cheese cut into pieces. Season to taste.

Put cabbage in casserole. Pour sauce over the cabbage. Top with crumbled potato chips.

Set in 350-degree oven and bake until mixture is bubbling. Serve hot.

Serves 6.

STUFFED CABBAGE ROLLS

1 head cabbage	1½ teaspoons salt
Boiling water	½ teaspoon black pepper
1 teaspoon fat	½ cup raw rice
1 onion, chopped	Green peppers (optional)
¼ cup hot fat	Sauerkraut (optional)
½ pound ground beef	1 No. 2 can tomatoes
½ pound ground fresh pork	Hot water

Wash cabbage, Remove 8 large leaves. Immerse these in boiling water to which 1 teaspoon fat has been added. When leaves have wilted, remove them. Set aside. When cool, you may want to slice off a bit of backbone or rib. This may be necessary to roll leaves without breaking them.

Sauté onion in hot fat. Add mixed meats, seasoning, and raw rice. Mix well. Chop remainder of head of cabbage. Prepare green peppers for stuffing at same time as cabbage, if desired.

Lay a cabbage leaf flat. Place large spoonful of meat mixture somewhat to left of center of leaf. Fold 1/3 of leaf over. Roll leaf. Tuck the outer ends of the leaf inside the roll. This makes a complete seal for the stuffing.

Fill peppers if desired.

Place 1/2 of the shredded cabbage in the bottom of a large kettle. Add sauerkraut if desired. Place cabbage rolls and peppers in kettle. Top with remaining shredded cabbage.

Pour tomatoes over top. Add enough hot water to bring liquid over rolls.

Cover kettle and simmer mixture for 1 1/2 to 2 hours.

Serves 6 to 8.

*   *   *

Additional recipes for cabbage will be found under Pickles and Relishes, Salads, Soups, and How To Freeze Vegetables.

Carrots

Dr. M. L. Lemery, physician to the King of England in 1740, wrote a *Treatise of all sorts of foods and drinkables*. He says of carrots: "Carots are roots much used in kitchens because of their taste which is agreeable enough. Carot in Latin is called Carrotta, from caro, 'flesh,' because 'tis as it were fleshy."

Saying their taste is agreeable enough is rather damning with faint praise. Today's nutritionists consider carrots an invaluable source of carotene or provitamin A.

Select carrots with deep orange flesh, since these contain maximum amounts of carotene. Remember that the deeper the yellow color the richer in vitamin A the vegetable.

Buying Guide: Smooth-textured; even tapering shape; flesh of good color; fresh in appearance. Condition of tops does not indicate quality of root, as tops are easily damaged and deteriorate rapidly.

[68]

Carrots with thick, excessive masses of leaf stems at neck usually have undesirably large cores; wilted, flabby, or shriveled roots are undesirable. Large, thick-necked, forked tips and cracked products undesirable.

Basic Rule for Cooking Carrots

Even when carrots are overcooked their vanity is not hurt. The color is still yellow or orange. But cooking for too long in too much water detracts from the flavor. Watch the cooking time.

Wash carrots well. Opinions differ as to whether the carrots should be scraped or pared before cooking. Modern usage does neither: carrots are cooked with their skins on. Gentle persuasion by your fingers gets the skins off a cooked carrot if it is held under running water. But slender tips are likely to break off in the process.

Bake well-washed carrots (no water added beyond that which clings to them) in heavy, tightly covered casserole in 300-degree oven. When carrots are baked, the flavor is well retained.

Or drop carrots, preferably whole, into rapidly boiling salted water.

Or cook carrots in pressure saucepan.

Or cook in a small amount of butter or margarine with a lettuce blanket French fashion (page 33).

And don't forget that young, sweet raw carrots may be cut into matchlike strips and served on a relish tray, or may be grated and added to many salads as another ingredient as well as an ornamental topping.

CARROTS WITH BUTTER

Cooked carrots freed from skins may be served with melted butter.

CARROTS WITH CREAM

Cooked carrots freed from skins may be dressed with a small amount of cream.

SAUTÉED CARROTS

Cooked carrots freed from skins may be sautéed lightly in butter.

CARROTS AND ONIONS

6 medium-sized carrots
1 bunch green onions
Butter or margarine

Wash and scrape carrots and cut into paper-thin slices. Cook briefly in boiling salted water. Do not overcook or carrot slices will be broken. Drain.

Cut onions, green tops and all, into small pieces. Sauté lightly.

Add carrots. Reheat and serve at once.

Serves 6.

CARROT LOAF

1 onion, sliced
2 tablespoons margarine
3 cups cooked carrots
½ cup chopped celery

1½ cups crumbed bread
2 eggs
¼ cup chopped parsley
Nutmeg

Sauté onion in margarine. Mash cooked carrots. Combine with remaining ingredients.

Put in greased loaf pan or casserole.

Bake in 350-degree oven for 40 minutes.

Serves 6.

FLEMISH CARROTS

8 carrots
2 tablespoons butter
½ teaspoon sugar
¼ cup water
Few grains nutmeg

1 cup cream
1 egg yolk
1 teaspoon finely chopped
    parsley

Parboil carrots in boiling salted water for 5 minutes. Remove skins. Slice into ½-inch-thick pieces.

Place butter, sugar, water, and nutmeg in saucepan. Add carrots. Simmer for 20 minutes.

Just before serving, add raw egg yolk mixed with cream and parsley. Reheat. Avoid boiling lest egg curdle.

Serve immediately.

Serves 4 to 6.

CARROTS WITH MINT GLAZE

20 small carrots
Boiling water
Salt

2 tablespoons butter
2 tablespoons sugar
4 or 5 sprigs fresh mint

Wash carrots and cook in boiling salted water. When tender, hold each carrot individually under the cold-water faucet and pull off the tender skin. It comes off almost like a glove.

Melt the butter in a heavy frying pan. Add the sugar. Into this buttery sirup put the carrots, whole or cut into halves lengthwise. Let them cook slowly until the surfaces are glazed.

The chopped mint may be sprinkled on after the glazing or added to the sirup when the carrots are put in.

Serves 6.

STEAMED PUDDING

1 cup ground carrots
1 cup ground potatoes
1 cup ground apples
1 cup ground suet
2 cups raisins
2 cups flour

1 cup sugar
1 teaspoon salt
1 teaspoon baking soda
1 teaspoon cinnamon
1 teaspoon nutmeg
¼ teaspoon cloves

Scrape raw carrots. Pare potatoes. Pare and core apples.

Put raw vegetables, apples, and suet through meat chopper, (coarse knife).

Wash and drain raisins. Sift flour, measure, and sift again with sugar, salt, soda, and spices. Combine mixtures.

Put in greased pudding pan. Steam for 3 hours.

Serve with lemon or hard sauce.

Serves 6.

*   *   *

Additional recipes for carrots will be found under Pickles and Relishes, Salads, Soups, and How To Freeze Vegetables.

Cauliflower

CAULIFLOWER was considered the aristocratic member of the cabbage family as long ago as the sixth century B.C. Even today it ranks high as a decorative vegetable, whether eaten raw or cooked.

Insects are likely to be found in the inner crevices or parts of the blossoming head. Invert the uncooked head in a salt-water solution to kill or draw out these tiny infestations.

BUYING GUIDE: Creamy white, tightly packed flowers with granular appearance. Size of head does not indicate quality. Leaves at base should be a fresh green. If flowerets spread or leaves are yellowed, the cauliflower is of inferior eating quality. Smudgy or speckled appearance often indicates presence of plant lice.

Basic Rule for Cooking Cauliflower

Cauliflower has an aristocratic look when properly cooked and served. Grandest of all is its entrance to the table

[73]

as a whole head topped with melted cheese, butter, and paprika.

Or consider and admire the cooked head with the same ruddy topping emerging from a surrounding rich cheese sauce held within bounds by the walls of a casserole.

Branching flowerets are often detached and cooked. They are good, too.

Put the cauliflower, head down, into boiling salted water. After 5 to 10 minutes reverse the position. The fleshy base requires a fair amount of time for cooking. The rising steam makes the blossom top tender.

Don't overcook, especially if you plan to put the whole head in the casserole and surround with the hot, well-flavored sauce. Cooking in the casserole set in a 350-degree oven continues for about 20 minutes.

BUTTERED CAULIFLOWER

Cooked flowerets may be dressed with melted butter made ruddy with paprika.

CAULIFLOWER WITH CREAM

Cooked flowerets may be dressed with cream.

CAULIFLOWER WITH CHEESE SAUCE

Whole head or flowerets may be cooked, drained, and dressed with rich cheese sauce.

GOLDEN CAULIFLOWER

1 cauliflower	Crumbs
Salt and pepper	Cooking oil
1 egg	Grated cheese

Separate cauliflower into flowerets that are not too small and cook them in boiling salted water until tender. Drain and cool. Season lightly with salt and pepper.

Dip flowerets in lightly beaten egg. Roll in crumbs, flour, or potato flour.

Sauté to a golden brown in cooking oil. Sprinkle generously with grated cheese and serve hot.

Serves 6.

VEGETABLE CUSTARD WITH HAM

1 cup cooked rice	2 eggs
4 or 5 carrots, cooked	2 cups milk
1 cup cooked peas	½ teaspoon salt
1 cauliflower, cooked	⅛ teaspoon paprika
1 slice ham, pan-fried and	1 tablespoon sherry
chopped	Garlic (optional)

Place a layer of rice in the bottom of a greased baking dish, then a layer of vegetables. Put chopped ham on vegetables. Top with rice.

Combine eggs, milk, and seasonings. Pour over the vegetables and meat. Pierce here and there with a fork to let custard seep through. Bake at 375 degrees for 50 to 60 minutes. Rub baking dish with garlic if desired.

Serves 6.

BAKED CAULIFLOWER AND CHEESE

1 head cauliflower	1 cup milk
4 tablespoons butter	½ cup cauliflower liquid
3 tablespoons flour	½ cup cheese
	2 tablespoons butter

Soak cauliflower in salted water. Cook in boiling salted water.

Make a white sauce of the butter, flour, and top milk (*See* page 219). Add ½ cup cauliflower liquid. Add ¼ cup cheese, cubed. Season.

Put vegetable in casserole. Pour sauce over it.

Dot with remaining cheese and butter. Sprinkle with paprika.

Bake until brown on top, about 35 minutes.

Serves 6.

*   *   *

Additional recipes for cauliflower will be found under Appetizers, Pickles and Relishes, Salads, Soups, and How To Freeze Vegetables.

Celeriac

THIS branch of the celery family develops enlarged underground roots. These are used in soups and stews. "Soup celery" is another name for celeriac.

BUYING GUIDE: Firm, clean.

Basic Rule for Cooking Celeriac

Wash in water. With a sharp knife, remove all traces of black dirt packed in the crevices of inner part of root. It may be necessary to cut the root apart to get it really clean.

Cook the cleaned root in boiling salted water, or add it to simmering soup stock, or to meat stew.

See Hot Celeriac Salad, page 208.

Celery

THE ANCIENTS considered celery a tonic for frazzled nerves. Less than fifty years ago, soda fountains served celery tonic, proving that that belief had held through the years. Regardless of its questionable ability to quiet nerves, celery is still a great favorite, because of its crunchiness and flavor. That flavor, incidentally, is more mild today than in ancient years. And vegetable growers are now producing celery that is tender but green, thereby increasing its vitamin content.

BUYING GUIDE: Tender, brittle, medium length and thickness, well-developed heart formation; inside of stem smooth.

There are two types of celery: Green, which has a smooth-textured stalk and a strong flavor; and yellow, which has slight ridges on the stalk and a much milder flavor. If stalks are unusually rough or puffy, celery is apt to be pithy. Avoid spotted yellow and brown leaves.

[78]

Basic Rule for Preparing Celery

Crisp, crunchy stalks of raw celery are what most people think of when they hear the word *celery*. But celery and its sister, celeriac, may be used to flavor soups and stews.

French chefs are masters at cooking celery. They braise it and bring it forth with pride as an excellent dinner vegetable.

Cut off root ends of stalks. Wash roots in running water, cutting them apart if necessary, to remove traces of black soil in which they grew.

Separate the stalks, washing each one, paying special attention to the grooves on the outer parts of the stalks. Cut off leafy tops (these may be added to soup, stews or the water in which chicken is cooked; or they may be chopped and used to flavor meat loaf). The inner stalks are the ones set aside to serve as a raw vegetable. The tougher outer stalks may be stripped of some of the stringy parts and be used for braising or other celery dishes.

Cut-up pieces of celery may be cooked, drained, and served as a plain vegetable. Don't overcook, especially if celery is put into pressure saucepan. During cooking, the vegetable seems to release salt, so do not put too much salt in the cooking water.

BUTTERED CELERY

Dress cooked, drained celery with melted butter.

CELERY IN CREAM

Dress cooked, drained celery with hot cream. Dust with paprika.

BRAISED CELERY

2 slices bacon, diced	8 celery stalks
1 onion, sliced	1 cup hot water
3 sprigs parsley	1 bouillon cube
Freshly crumbed bread	

Cut bacon into dice, using scissors. Place bacon, sliced onion, and parsley in bottom of shallow baking dish. Cover with cleaned celery stalks.

Dissolve bouillon cube in hot water. Pour over celery.

Set uncovered baking dish in 325-degree oven. Bake for 45 minutes.

Sauté freshly crumbed bread in small amount of butter. Sprinkle over celery during last 20 minutes of baking.

VARIATION: Tomato paste or chopped garlic may be added to bacon. Oil may be substituted for bacon.

Serves 4.

SCALLOPED HAM AND CELERY WITH CHEESE

1 cup chopped celery
2 tablespoons butter
2 tablespoons flour
1½ cups chicken broth or cream

¼ teaspoon salt
1 cup chopped ham
Grated cheese
Paprika

Parboil celery.

Melt butter, add flour, and cook until bubbling. Add broth or cream and stir continually until thickened and smooth. Boil 2 minutes. Season.

Place ham and celery in alternate layers in a buttered baking dish and top with the sauce. Cover the top with a generous layer of cheese. Dust with paprika. Place in 350-degree oven until cheese is melted.

Serves 6.

*   *   *

Additional recipes for celery will be found under Appetizers, Pickles and Relishes, Salads, and Soups.

*   *   *

CHARD (*see* Swiss Chard, page 166).

CHICORY, BOTH CURLY AND WITLOOF (*see* Endive, page 96).

CHINESE CABBAGE OR CHINESE CELERY (*see* Cabbage, page 63).

This vegetable is usually sliced crosswise and added raw to green salads. It may be sliced crosswise and cooked like celery.

CHIVES, belonging to the onion family, are sold in red-clay pots. The rich green shoots practically fill the pots, growing with great rapidity.

Because of the large amount of surface exposed and the rapid growth the plant needs almost daily watering.

Use scissors to cut off the shoots used in salads or for garnish or flavor.

When the plant tops have been sheared again and again, transplant the chives into the garden. Here they take a new lease on life. Before too long you will have a flourishing clump of chives.

BUYING GUIDE: Shoots about 3½ to 4 inches in height; dark rich green; fresh-looking. Avoid pots with tall shoots straw-colored at tips.

Chives improve almost any vegetable dish. Use them freely.

Collards

THE ANGLO-SAXON name for this leafy green vegetable was "coleworts." Breaking down the word, we know that *cole* put the vegetable in the cabbage family. *Wort* means roots. However, it is the leaves of collards that are cooked and used as greens. Collards and kale are kinds of cabbage which form no head. All growth goes into the large green leaves.

BUYING GUIDE: Crisp and fresh, free from insect injury indicated by leaf perforations. Yellowing and wilted leaves indicate age or damage.

Cook as directed for kale (page 101).

Corn, Sweet

WITHOUT doubt, Americans are the greatest sweet-corn growers and eaters in the world. Popular varieties are Golden Bantam, Country Gentleman, Stowell's Mexican. No other vegetable loses its distinctive and delicious flavor as rapidly as corn once it has been picked from the stalk.

BUYING GUIDE: Fresh green husks, bright, plump, milky kernels. No space between rows. Ears filled to tips. Silk dry and dark brown. Yellowed dry husks indicate age or damage. Tiny soft kernels indicate immature corn. Worm injury not serious if confined to tips.

Basic Rules for Cooking Corn

Once more, we stress the necessity of the briefest of interims between buying, cooking, and serving this favorite American vegetable.

Remove outer husks. Remove clinging corn-silk strands. A small vegetable brush simplifies the removal of corn silk. Cut out any diseased or worm-eaten parts. Extreme tip of ear may be broken off. Large ears may be broken crosswise into halves.

CORN ON THE COB

If pressure saucepan is large enough the ears may be cooked in that. Or a large kettle of water may be brought to boiling while the ears are being husked. A spoon or two of sugar may be added to the water.

Put ears in water, submerging them. After water comes back to boil allow approximately 8 minutes' cooking time.

Remove from boiling water. Serve hot corn at once. Butter and salt are the usual accompaniments.

CORN MEXICAN

Kernels may be cut from cooked ears. Combine them with a small amount of coarsely chopped pimiento and green pepper.

Sauté the mixture in hot fat. Strips of bacon may be cooked, cut into pieces, and added to the corn. In this case the sautéing is done in the bacon fat. Season well.

ROASTED EARS

In many parts of the country, an outdoor picnic is not complete without "roastin' ears." Actually, they are likely to be overrated. Cooking in hot embers tends to overcook, even to char, some of the kernels.

The basic method calls for (1) immersion of unhusked ears in deep pails of water (2) wrapping of wet, unhusked ears in thick folds of wet newspapers; (3) burying of these bundles under glowing embers.

The wet newspaper and husks are slowly dried, creating steam in the process. This steam cooks the corn. The ears should be removed from the hot embers before the paper or husks are so dry they catch fire.

SWEET CORN WAFFLES

1 cup sweet corn pulp
½ teaspoon salt
1 teaspoon sugar
2 eggs, beaten

¾ cup milk
1 tablespoon melted butter
2 cups flour
3 teaspoons baking powder

With a small, sharp knife, score down the rows of kernels on cobs of sweet corn, then with the blunt edge of the knife press out the pulp, until there is enough to make 1 cup. Season with salt, sugar, eggs, milk, and melted butter. Sift flour with baking powder and add to the first mixture. More flour may be necessary if the pulp is watery; enough should be used to get the consistency of waffle batter: that is, one which will quickly find its level when poured. Cook in waffle iron.

Serves 4 to 6.

CORN OYSTERS

½ cup flour
1 teaspoon salt
¼ teaspoon monosodium
  glutamate

2 cups corn cut from cob
2 eggs, separated

Sift and measure flour. Add salt and monosodium glutamate. Sift. Combine corn and egg yolks. Add to first mixture. Fold in stiffly beaten whites.

Cook by spoonfuls in small amount of fat in a heavy frying pan.

Serves 4 to 6.

CORN FRITTERS

1 cup flour
¼ teaspoon salt
2/3 cup milk
2 eggs, separated

1 tablespoon melted butter
½ cup corn, canned or cut
  from the cob

Sift and measure flour. Add salt. Sift again.

Combine milk and beaten yolks. Add to flour. Mix well. Add melted butter. Add corn. Fold in stiffly beaten egg whites.

Drop by spoonfuls into deep fat, heated to 375 degrees. Fry until delicate brown (about 4 minutes). Remove from fat, drain, and put on crumpled paper.

Serve hot with maple sirup.

Serves 6.

SUCCOTASH

6 ears corn
1 pint Lima beans
1 cup top milk

1 cup cream
2 tablespoons butter
Salt, pepper

Remove husks and silk from ears of corn. With a sharp knife, cut off the tops of the kernels. Put these to cook in a small amount of boiling water. In the meantime, remove the milky part of the kernels by rubbing the dull edge of a table knife up and down the rows of kernels which have had their tops cut off. Add the milky pulp to the kernel tops and cook for about 5 minutes longer.

Cook the Lima beans in rapidly boiling salted water.

Combine cooked corn with cooked Lima beans, having about twice as much corn as beans.

Add milk and cream. Season with salt, pepper, and butter.

Serves 6.

CORN ALAMO

2 tablespoons fat
3 tablespoons chopped onion
3 tablespoons chopped green
    pepper

2 cups corn cut from cob
3 tablespoons water
¾ teaspoon salt
⅛ teaspoon pepper

Melt fat in frying pan. Add onion and green pepper. Cook over medium heat for 5 minutes.

Add corn, water, and seasonings and cover pan. Cook another 10 minutes over medium heat. Serve hot.

Serves 4.

CORN PUDDING

2 cups milk
2 eggs, slightly beaten
2 cups corn, cooked
1 teaspoon sugar
1½ tablespoons melted butter

1 teaspoon salt
⅛ teaspoon pepper
2 tablespoons chopped green pepper

Mix in order given and bake at 350 degrees for about 1 hour, or until custard is set.

The chopped green pepper is optional.

Serves 6.

*   *   *

Additional recipes for corn will be found under Pickles and Relishes, Soups, and Home Canning of Vegetables.

Cucumbers

Sᴀʏs Sairey Gamp in *Martin Chuzzlewit:*

I think young woman, that I could pick a little bit of pickled salmon with a nice sprig of fennel and a sprinkling of white pepper. I takes new bread, my dear, with just a little pat of fresh butter and a mossel of cheese. In case there should be such a thing as a cowcumber in the house will you be so kind as to bring it, for I'm rather partial to 'em, and they does a world of good in a sick room.

The pronunciation has changed since Dickens' day and nutritionists may question the "world of good" cucumbers can do in a sickroom. At one time, the cucumber was pared, sliced, soaked in salt water, wrung out until it was a limp rag: only then was it considered safe to eat. Now we leave the skin on and serve a vegetable crunchy and delicious to the last bite.

Cucumbers in all shapes, sizes, and forms are pickled. Only the commercial pickle maker has the "know how," the equipment, and the controlled environment to change whole cucumbers into firm, well-flavored pickles. Excellent sliced or chunk pickles are the kinds best made at home.

BUYING GUIDE: Smooth, firm, glossy, and dark green; medium size with uniform diameter; ends blunt and rounded; seeds immature. Beware of cucumbers which are dull, yellowed, rubbery, and tough. Decay appears anywhere on surface as a dark, sunken area.

Basic Rules for Preparing Cucumbers

Perky, crisp cucumbers are in great contrast to the limp, tough slices that were served by Great Grandmama. She cut off and discarded a thick peeling. She used a slaw cutter to get wafer-thin slices, which were heavily salted. After an hour or so the slices were literally wrung out of the brine. Then they were dressed with heavy sour cream and black pepper. They were good, too, with fried potatoes country style.

Such cucumbers may find their place on a *smörgåsbord* table. But by and large today's cucumber is treated more gently.

Wash cucumber. Run sharp tines of fork up and down the skin surface of the cucumber. When the cucumber is sliced these markings give the dark green skin the appearance of cogs on a pale green wheel.

About ½ inch at the bottom and top of a cucumber is discarded. All the rest is used.

Sometimes the unpeeled cucumber is cut into long narrow wedges that appear in pleasing contrast to raw carrot sticks and pale-ivory celery hearts.

SWEET AND SOUR CUCUMBERS

2 cucumbers   2 tablespoons sugar
¼ cup water   3 tablespoons vinegar
½ cup sour cream   Salt and pepper
1 egg yolk   Paprika

Peel cucumbers and cut into thick slices. Cook these in water until water is absorbed and cucumber is browned.

Mix sour cream, egg yolk, sugar, vinegar, and seasonings. Pour mixture over cucumbers.

Cook over low flame until mixture boils up once. Remove from fire immediately and serve.

Serves 6.

COTTAGE CUCUMBERS

1 cup cottage cheese   ¼ cup green pepper, chopped
1½ cups crumbed bread   1 tablespoon butter
½ cup sour cream   Salt
1 tablespoon parsley   6 cucumbers

Mix cottage cheese, bread crumbs, sour cream, and parsley. Sauté the chopped green pepper in butter until soft, but not browned. Add to cheese mixture and season with salt.

Hollow out center of peeled cucumbers. Cut lengthwise. Put cheese mixture in each half. Put in greased baking dish.

Bake at 375 degrees for 25 minutes, or until cucumbers are tender.

May be served with tomato sauce.

Serves 6.   *   *   *

Additional recipes for cucumbers will be found under Appetizers, Pickles and Relishes, Salads, How To Freeze Vegetables, and Home Canning of Vegetables.

*   *   *

DANDELION GREENS (*see* Greens, page 99).

Eggplant

Glossy purple skin and a shape like an oversized egg or pear identify this vegetable, which has been accepted for table use only recently. It is a "Johnny-come-lately" edible vegetable, although its known history goes back to the early centuries before the Christian era.

In this country, for a long time eggplant was considered ornamental but not edible. Finally some brave soul tried slicing and paring it and sprinkling it generously with salt. The slices were piled under a heavy plate for an hour or so (to draw out the poisonous juices). The vegetable was then considered safe to be cooked and eaten. Today, it is known that no juice contained within the vegetable is poisonous.

BUYING GUIDE: Uniform dark glossy purple color; heavy, smooth, firm; pear- or egg-shaped; three to six inches in diameter. Shriveled and flabby ones undesirable. Decay appears as a dark, sunken, irregular area on surface.

Basic Rule for Cooking Eggplant

Well-cooked eggplant should have a crusty exterior with a soft, tender pulp within. This rule applies to the vegetable when sliced and sautéed or cut into strips and fried in deep fat. Americans are likely to use these two methods.

Peoples of the Near and Far East cook the vegetable differently. Sometimes they may stuff it with meat and season it well, thereby using the eggplant as a flavor extender of meat.

The Italians usually sauté slices in olive oil and then cook these pieces with herbs, nutmeats, or crumbs and with plenty of tomato paste, making a rich dish with a dusky look and an exotic flavor.

SAUTÉED EGGPLANT SLICES

Wash eggplant. Cut into slices about ¾ inch thick. Pare these slices if preferred (today's tendency is to leave the skins on).

Sprinkle salt lightly on cut surfaces and pile slices atop one another. Press down under a weighted plate. Let stand for an hour or so.

Coat each slice with flour to which a little monosodium glutamate has been added.

Heat heavy frying pan or griddle. Have about ¼ inch melted fat on hot surface. Lay slices on griddle. Cook over moderate heat until one side is browned. Turn slices and brown other side. By this time, the slices have lost their chalky look and are almost quivery in texture.

Serve at once.

OVEN SAUTÉED EGGPLANT SLICES

Prepare as for griddle sautéeing. Set in 350-degree oven. Slices get brown and crusty in about 20 minutes.

DEEP FAT FRIED EGGPLANT STICKS

Cut raw eggplant into 3-inch lengths. Have pieces about ⅓ inch thick. Roll in seasoned flour or finely sifted dry crumbs. Cook in frying basket immersed in deep fat heated to 375 degrees. Take out as soon as surface is brown. Overcooking makes sticks dry.

ELEGANT EGGPLANT

1 large eggplant, sliced	Cooking oil
4 tomatoes, sliced	Salt
½ onion, chopped	Black pepper, freshly ground
½ green pepper, shredded	*Orégano* and basil (few sprigs)

Wash eggplant and cut in ½-inch-thick slices. Pare slices. Wash, skin, and cut tomatoes in ½ inch thick slices.

Sauté chopped onion and shredded green pepper in small amount of cooking oil. Remove from oil.

Sauté eggplant slices (more oil will be needed).

Place layer of eggplant, then one of tomatoes, in casserole. Dot with onion and green pepper. Season with salt and freshly ground black pepper. Add few sprigs of fresh *orégano* and sweet basil. Repeat, finishing with eggplant slices on top.

Cover casserole. Set in 375-degree oven. Bake until eggplant slices are tender, uncovering the casserole during the latter part of baking.

Serves 4 to 6.

BAKED STUFFED EGGPLANT

1 eggplant	1 cup deviled ham
¼ cup chopped onion	1 egg
2 tablespoons margarine	¼ cup grated cheese
½ cup crumbed potato chips	

Parboil whole, unpared eggplant for 10 minutes. Cut in half lengthwise. Scoop out pulp, leaving a 1-inch wall.

Cut pulp in small pieces. Sauté onion in margarine. Combine with eggplant pulp, deviled ham, and beaten egg.

Fill shells, top with cheese and potato chips. Bake at 375 degrees for 25 minutes.

Serves 4 to 6.

EGGPLANT PARMIGIANA

1 large eggplant
1 cup olive oil
1¼ cups tomato sauce
1¼ cups Italian tomato sauce
  (page 222)

3 tablespoons grated Parmesan
  cheese
½ pound Mozzarella cheese,
  sliced thin

Peel eggplant and cut into ½ inch thick slices. Sauté them in oil until brown and drain well on paper.

Place one layer of eggplant in casserole. Cover with Italian tomato sauce. Sprinkle with Parmesan cheese. Cover with a layer of Mozzarella cheese. Repeat procedure until all eggplant is used, ending with Mozzarella cheese.

Bake in a 400-degree oven for 15 minutes.

Serves 4 to 6.

*   *   *

Additional recipes for eggplant will be found under How To Freeze Vegetables and Home Canning of Vegetables.

Endive

APPARENTLY what name you give endive, escarole, and chicory depends on the part of the country from which you come.

Curly endive is related to chicory and often confused therewith. This green shapes itself into loose, wide-spreading heads which have been bleached to a buttery color at the center, shading to dark green toward the outer part. The leaves have serrated or ragged edges that tend to curl somewhat, giving a fringed appearance. The flavor is slightly bitter, especially in the outer leaves.

Batavian endive, sometimes called "escarole," has leaves that are broad and flat rather than curled at the tips.

Witloof chicory or French endive has always been considered a delicacy. The head is made of tightly fitting, smooth, long leaves which have been bleached to the palest of yellow-green.

But remember, your greengrocer may call these three vegetables any of the names given above.

BUYING GUIDE: *See* Greens (page 100).

*   *   *

ESCAROLE *(see* Endive, page 96).

Seed catalogues describe this vegetable as a broad-leaved endive. It is well-rounded and compact. It is used mostly for salads.

Fennel or Finocchio

THE ITALIANS use large amounts of fennel, which they call *finocchio*. The fleshy root of one variety is cooked and eaten as a vegetable. Perhaps the most popular use of feathery fennel is in fish dishes.

BUYING GUIDE: Similar in appearance to celery. Tender white bulb with no blemishes; bright green featherlike leaves. Bulb should not be rough or puffy.

BRAISED FENNEL

2 pounds fennel (bulbous part)
1/3 cup butter
Monosodium glutamate
1 teaspoon salt
1 cup meat stock
Pepper

Wash and scrape fennel. Cut into 1-inch pieces. Sauté in butter until lightly brown.

Add salt, meat stock, pepper, and monosodium glutamate. Cook until tender.

NOTE: Meat stock may be canned consommé, used undiluted. If canned consommé is used, omit the salt called for in the recipe.

Serves 6.

Greens

THE USES to which greens are put varies. Some leafy greens are always cooked; some are found only in salads; some are used both raw and cooked.

(1) Leafy greens used RAW in salads: Chicory, Chinese cabbage or Chinese celery, endive, escarole, lettuce, parsley, romaine, watercress.

(2) Leafy greens usually COOKED before serving: Beet greens, collards, dandelion greens, kale, mustard greens, spinach, turnip tops or greens.

(3) Leafy greens served either RAW or COOKED: Chinese cabbage, young dandelion leaves, lamb's quarters, young mustard greens, young spinach.

Basic Rule for Leafy Green Preparation

(a) *Cleaning:* Leafy vegetables grow close to the ground. This means that a good deal of sand and dirt may be on them, especially if they have been gathered shortly after a rain. Biting down on grains of sand destroys eating pleasure.

How best can you get the sand off the leaves? The answer is *wash* and *wash* and *wash again*. Use gently running warm water. If you put the greens in a pan, be sure to lift them from the pan before you drain the water. Sand seems to be drawn toward the leaves as though they were magnets. Cut or break off roots or rootlets. Remove all bruised or decayed leaves. Strip stiff midribs and discard them.

(b) *Cooking:* Put leaves, with such water as is clinging to them, in a colander. Set this over a pan of boiling water. Cover the greens. Within a few minutes the steam will have wilted or tenderized the leaves. Do not overcook them or they will look dingy, limp, and discouraged. Cut cooked greens with kitchen scissors if they look unwieldy. Season. Put in hot serving dish. Serve at once.

BUYING GUIDE: Bright-green color; tender, crisp leaves; minimum of tough stems and of dirt. Avoid wilted leaves or heads. Watch for insects in and on under-side of leaves.

*   *   *

Recipes for greens will be found under Salads and Home Canning of Vegetables.

Kale

Two MEMBERS of the cabbage family are nonheading. Both kale and collards are believed to resemble cabbage as it was when grown without cultivation centuries ago. The leaves are fairly heavy and deeply frilled. They need to be stripped from the tough stalks. The flavor is rather strong.

BUYING GUIDE: Well-curled, crisp, dark or bluish-green leaves. Some kale has a brownish cast, which is not attractive but which is no detriment to flavor. Avoid wilted or yellow leaves and excess dirt.

SCALLOPED KALE

3 cups cooked kale (4 pounds fresh)	1 cup white sauce (page 219)
3 eggs	1 cup grated cheese

Cook kale in boiling salted water.

Hard-cook and chop the eggs. Arrange the kale, eggs, white sauce, and grated cheese in layers in a casserole or baking dish.

Bake at 400 degrees for 15 minutes, or until bubbling.

Serves 6.

Kohlrabi

THE NAME "kohlrabi" is self-explanatory to students of languages. *Kohl* identifies it as belonging to the cabbage family; *rabi* relates it to the turnip. And that is exactly what the vegetable is: a hybrid cabbage-turnip.

Shaped like a turnip, the vegetable shows itself above ground with pale-green long-stemmed leaves sprouting out at intervals around its sides.

The flavor is rather mild, lacking both the pungent bite of cabbage and the earthy flavor of turnip.

BUYING GUIDE: Select small- to medium-sized kohlrabi showing a bit of root stem, heavy for size, firm with edible tops, fresh, tender, medium-sized leaves of a good green color. Beware of oversized bulbs.

Basic Rule for Cooking Kohlrabi

Kohlrabi is neither well known nor popular throughout the United States. Home gardeners are likely to let the bulbous vegetable get too old before using it. The result is a woody mass without much flavor.

Caught and used young, kohlrabi makes a welcome change from—or addition to—the usual assortment of vegetables.

Wash bulbs. Pare. Cut into cubes. Cook in boiling salted water to which a small amount of monosodium glutamate has been added. Drain and serve hot.

BUTTERED KOHLRABI

Dress cooked, cubed kohlrabi with melted butter.

Why not experiment with the various leafy herbs to see what one or more of them will do for this mild-flavored vegetable?

KOHLRABI IN CREAM

Drain hot cooked cubes or slices. Add cream and dusting of paprika.

RAW KOHLRABI

Wash and pare kohlrabi and cut into wafer-thin slices. Serve with raw carrot sticks, celery, and green onions on relish tray.

Try dipping slices into Green Goddess Dip for Chips (page 186).

*   *   *

See also How To Freeze Vegetables.

*   *   *

LAMB'S QUARTERS (*see* Greens, page 99).

Leeks

THIS mildly flavored member of the onion family might almost qualify as Caspar Milquetoast, distantly related to the onion branch. Perhaps its mild flavor accounts for its use as a food since prehistoric days. Egypt is reported to have grown some of the best-flavored leeks. They are mentioned in the Bible: "We remember the fish which we did eat in Egypt freely; the cucumbers and the melons and the leeks and the onions and the garlic." In one of the decisive battles between the Welsh and the Saxons, the men from Wales, who won, wore leek plants on their helmets. They attributed their victory to this decoration. To this day, the leek is the national symbol of Wales. It is of same rank as the thistle of Scotland, the shamrock of Ireland, and the rose of England.

BUYING GUIDE: *See* Onions, page 115.

Basic Rule for Cooking Leeks

Occasionally leeks may appear as a vegetable dish in their own right. In such a case, they are washed. The flat, bulb-like base and about 3 inches of the joining flat green stems are cooked in boiling salted water, drained, and served with butter.

Leeks are used to add flavor to vegetable soups. They are much used today because of the great popularity of Vichyssoise, that smooth as satin cream soup which is made of a little potato, some leeks, much chicken broth, cream, and butter.

*　　*　　*

See also Vichyssoise Crème, page 238.

Lettuce

BREAK apart a stalk of lettuce and you notice a milky liquid. That liquid is supposed to explain the name "lettuce" for this most popular of salad plants. *Laitues* is Old French for "milky."

The Latin name for lettuce is *lactuca,* closely related to the Latin word for milk, which is *lac.*

All of which points to the world-wide growth of lettuce. The early kinds, it is believed, grew wild. That means they were not as tender, well-shaped, or gentle-flavored as the varieties grown today.

Perhaps the most highly favored one today is Bibb Lettuce. If you have not eaten any thus far, keep asking for it at your greengrocer's. You will be amply repaid when you taste it.

BUYING GUIDE: Head lettuce or iceberg lettuce should be round, firm, and heavy for size, with crisp, tender leaves. It should be medium green on the outside with a pale green heart.

The Butterhead variety of lettuce has a soft, light-weight head which is not as crisp in texture as iceberg, but it is very tender. It should have light-green outer leaves and light-yellow leaves inside.

Bibb Lettuce, a variety of Butterhead, is considered the aristocrat of lettuces. It is tender and definitely good eating. Boston Lettuce is another variety of Butterhead.

Cos lettuce or romaine has coarse, medium-green leaves; the head is moderately firm and elongated.

Leaf lettuce has numerous bright-green, coarse-textured, heavily crimped leaves, which are attached to a short central stem.

The preparation of lettuce is discussed at length under Salads (page 196). Another use for lettuce is pointed out on page 196, where the French provincial method of cooking fresh vegetables is given in detail.

See Salads, Soups.

Mushrooms

Botanically speaking, mushrooms are not vegetables but fungi. However, the men who grow vegetables under glass count mushrooms as one of their products. Those mushrooms which have been cultivated are edible, whereas only an expert can differentiate between poisonous and nonpoisonous wild ones.

Buying Guide: Short, thick, firm stems; white velvety caps. Caps should not be discolored, pitted, or shriveled.

Hothouse-grown mushrooms seldom require washing or peeling. The stem ends may be tough and can be discarded or pared before using.

Basic Rule for Cooking Mushrooms

Don't be alarmed when fresh mushrooms change color from a puttylike gray to a dark, almost black, brown. This change occurs during cooking and is to be expected.

On the other hand, button mushrooms which have been

canned commercially retain their original appearance. They are quite hard and rubbery in texture, whereas fresh ones are comparatively soft and tender when cooked.

The skin of hothouse-grown mushrooms is so tender no peeling is required.

The stem, short as it is, is quite woody. You may want to peel or cut off the outer part. These outer parts may be simmered in water to make a mushroom-flavored liquid which may be added when making mushroom dishes, or when diluting commercially canned mushroom soup.

SAUTÉED MUSHROOM CAPS

Put whole or halved caps in butter or margarine which has been melted in a heavy frying pan. Cover the pan and let the mushrooms cook slowly for about 15 minutes. Some juices exude from the mushrooms as they cook. Therefore less butter is required than would be necessary if the mushrooms remained dry.

CREAMED MUSHROOMS

After mushrooms have been simmering in melted butter and their own juices for 15 minutes or so, pour on a small amount of cream. This blends with the juices, making a rich mixture, which may be served on toast. To extend the amount, use more cream. In this case you may need to thicken the liquid with a little flour. Sprinkle this over the sautéed mushrooms before adding the cream. The mixture thickens as it simmers.

STUFFED MUSHROOM CAPS

12 large mushroom caps
¼ cup deviled ham
2 tablespoons fresh tomato
  pulp

3 tablespoons freshly crumbed
  bread
Chopped chives
Seasoning

1 tablespoon cream

Sauté mushroom caps in small amount of butter over low heat. After 5 minutes' cooking, remove and set aside.

Combine remaining ingredients. Mix well. Put mounds of mixture in each mushroom cap.

Set in hot oven for few minutes, or brown under broiler heat.

Serves 6.

CREAMED MUSHROOMS WITH GREEN BEANS

¼ cup butter   1 cup sweet cream
1 pound mushrooms   1 cup sour cream
1 cup cooked green beans   Seasonings
3 tablespoons flour   ¼ cup sherry (optional)

Melt ⅛ cup butter in heavy frying pan. Remove stems from mushroom caps and sauté mushroom caps and peeled stems slowly in butter. When soft, add drained cooked beans.

Make a roux of ⅛ cup of butter and flour. When bubbling, add sweet cream slowly. When smooth and bubbling add sour cream, mushrooms, and beans. Heat lightly. Season to taste. Before serving, add sherry, if desired.

Cooked coarsely chopped chestnuts may be substituted for beans.

Crunchy potato chips are an excellent accompaniment.

Serves 4.

*   *   *

Additional recipes for mushrooms will be found under Soups, How To Freeze Vegetables, and Home Canning of Vegetables.

Okra

Cʜɪᴄᴋᴇɴ gumbo soup is a favorite in Louisiana. Philadelphia Pepper Pot Soup is a Northern favorite. Both of these soups have a mucilaginous quality from the use of okra, one of the ingredients.

This vegetable matures within a week after the pods start developing. The pods look like closed but unrolled pale-green umbrellas with a roughened texture. A cut slice reveals the fleshy ribs and seeds, both sticky to the touch.

Bᴜʏɪɴɢ Gᴜɪᴅᴇ: Green or white in color; long and thin or short and stocky; pods that snap easily.

Basic Rule for Cooking Okra

Southerners who have been brought up where okra is a vegetable in common use are better judges of it than other people. They stress the need for using okra while it is young and tender. They also call attention to the rapidity with which the okra pods mature once they have taken shape on the plant.

Wash okra pods, which should not be more than 2½ inches long. Cut off stem, but do not cut into pod while doing this.

Cook in boiling salted water until pods are tender but not soft or mushy. Drain.

BUTTERED OKRA

Dress hot okra pods with melted butter. A little lemon juice or herbal vinegar may be added to the melted butter.

OKRA WITH HOLLANDAISE SAUCE

Cook and drain okra. Serve hot with a spoonful of Hollandaise sauce spooned over each serving.

OKRA STUFFED GREEN PEPPERS

1 large onion, sliced	1 cup water
¼ cup bacon fat	Salt, pepper
6 tomatoes	6 green peppers
1 quart okra	Buttered crumbs

Sauté an onion in bacon fat. Add sliced raw tomatoes, okra pods, and boiling water. Let mixture simmer for an hour. Season to taste. Fill green-pepper cases with this mixture. Top with buttered crumbs. Bake until the crumbs are browned.

OKRA AND LAMB STEW

1 pound lamb	8 okra
2 tablespoons margarine	Salt and pepper
2 onions, sliced	6 leaves fresh thyme *or*
1 cup lamb broth	⅛ teaspoon crumbled dry
2 cups tomato juice	thyme

Purchase boneless lamb for stew. Cook lamb in water to cover until tender. Remove meat. Cut in small pieces. Sauté meat and onions in margarine.

Cook broth down to 1 cup. Add tomato juice.

Wash okra. Cut off stem ends. Cut in thick slices. Add to broth. Add salt, pepper, and thyme. Simmer for 30 minutes.

Add meat and onions. Heat to boiling. Serve with boiled rice.

Serves 6.

OKRA AND TOMATOES

3 onions	½ pound okra
3 tablespoons bacon fat	2 cups chopped tomatoes
2 green peppers	½ teaspoon salt

Slice onions and sauté in bacon fat a minute or two. Add chopped peppers and cook another minute. Add remaining ingredients and cook, covered, about 10 minutes.

Remove cover and continue cooking a few minutes longer, until okra is tender.

Fresh corn cut from the cob may be added.

Serves 6.

*   *   *

Additional recipes for okra will be found under Soups, How To Freeze Vegetables, and Home Canning of Vegetables.

Onions

Onions, garlic, leeks, chives, scallions, and shallots are members of the lily family. The flavors of all of them are related, varying in intensity from assertive garlic to gentle, persuasive leeks.

Spring onions or green onions or scallions are eaten stem, insignificant bulb, and all. Only the hollow spears of chives are eaten.

So-called "dry" onions are used for the flavor they give to food. Papery-skinned white ones vary in shape and size. When round, and about an inch in diameter, they are cooked and served buttered, creamed, or glazed.

The large, flat-bulbed, white-fleshed Spanish and Bermuda onions are juicy and sweet. They are used raw in salads. So are the more peppery dark, red-fleshed Italian ones.

Onions are an excellent example of the Doctrine of Signatures so popular in the Middle Ages. People believed that a Beneficent Creator fashioned growing things to show their medicinal value. How else could those first doctors have known which plants could cure what? The hollow stem of the onion resembles the hollow "pipes" in man that lead from head down toward chest and lungs. Humans suffered from colds in the chest; throats were raw and sore. The cure was obvious: a concoction made from that hollow-stemmed plant the onion. Sirup of onions and onion poultices are still used as a home remedy.

BUYING GUIDE: Domestic and Bermuda onions should be glossy, even-shaped, and dry enough to crackle, with hard bulbs and thin necks. Those with sprouts or a soggy feel are undesirable.

Scallions, green onions, leeks, and shallots: bleached stems to about three inches from roots. Shallots are generally red in color with good bright-green tops. Watch for freshness.

Chives are rich-green hollow spears which grow in a compact plant. This member of the onion family is used exclusively as an herb.

Basic Rule for Cooking Onions

'Twould be fine if a workable rule for avoiding tears when preparing onions could be given. But none of the methods suggested work for all people. "Weep no more, my lady" cannot be promised.

In the case of cooking onions, where the outer skin is brown in color, it is essential that this skin be removed. You may want to try cooking white-skinned onions with the skin left on. After cooking, it may be removed. If it were left on, you would find the onion difficult to eat, since the skin becomes exceedingly tough.

Some people start at the base, others at the stem end, to

remove the outer skin. A sharp-pointed knife and patience are both required.

Boiling salted water in a larger amount than used for other vegetables is needed for onions. Their cooking time is comparatively long, due to their compact form.

BUTTERED ONIONS

Mild white onions, about 1½ inches in diameter, should be used. Drain after cooking. Dress with melted butter and finely chopped parsley.

CREAMED ONIONS

Dress drained cooked onions with a thin white sauce (page 220). Dust with paprika.

STUFFED ONIONS

> 6 Spanish onions
> Boiling salted water
> 2 cups consommé

Stuffing

¼ pound sausage meat	1 cup freshly crumbed bread
2 tablespoons diced celery	1 cup fresh tomato pulp
Parboiled onion centers	1 tablespoon minced parsley

Seasonings

Remove papery skin from onions. Cook onions in boiling salted water for 30 minutes. Drain and cool. Remove onion centers, leaving onion walls about ¾ inch thick.

Prepare stuffing. Cook sausage meat until lightly browned. Remove meat. Sauté diced celery and onion centers, which have been chopped, in the hot fat. Add fresh tomato pulp, crumbed bread, minced parsley. Add cooked sausage meat. Mix well. Season to taste.

Stuff onions. Place stuffed onions in baking dish. Set in 350-degree oven. Baste with consommé during the baking. Baking takes 1 to 1½ hours. Onions should be tender when pierced with a sharp-tined fork.

Serves 6.

ONIONS AND APPLES

4 Bermuda onions   3 tablespoons butter
2 apples, cored   Salt
                    Sugar

Peel onions and slice.

Leave skins on cored apples. Slice into ¼ inch thick slices.

Place butter in frying pan. Arrange layers of apples and of onions.

Sprinkle lightly with salt. If desired, about 2 tablespoons of sugar may be sprinkled on top.

Cook over low fire until onions and apples are soft.

Serves 6.

GLAZED ONIONS

2 pounds white onions   6 tablespoons sugar
½ cup melted butter   Paprika

Boil peeled onions in salted water for 20 to 40 minutes, or until onions are tender.

Heat butter in a heavy frying pan. Add onions. Sprinkle with sugar. Cook over low heat about 10 minutes, or until onions are glazed, turning them frequently. Sprinkle with paprika.

NOTE: For honey-glazed onions, decrease sugar to 2 tablespoons; add ¼ cup honey and 2 tablespoons lemon juice.

Serves 6.

ONIONS DE LUXE

12 to 15 white onions	12 to 15 cloves
3 tablespoons butter or margarine	3 tablespoons margarine
2 tablespoons sugar	4 tablespoons flour
	1 cup chicken broth

1 cup milk or cream

Select medium-sized white onions. Remove outer, papery skin. Cook onions until almost done in boiling, salted water. They should hold their shape and still be slightly hard.

Drain the onions. Melt butter in frying pan. Add sugar and let the two cook to a sirup. Insert a whole clove in each onion. Now glaze onions in the butter-sugar, turning frequently, until they are light brown.

Put onions in the baking dish. Make cream sauce, using both milk and chicken broth for liquid (*see* page 221). Pour sauce over onions and let them cook until the mixture is bubbling. Serve hot.

Serves 6.

FRENCH FRIED ONIONS

4 large sweet onions (Bermuda or Spanish)	Milk
	Seasoned flour

Deep fat

·Wash and peel onions and cut into 1/4-inch slices. Let stand in milk to cover for 1 hour. Drain.

Roll in flour seasoned with salt, pepper, monosodium glutamate.

Heat fat to 375 degrees. Put a few slices at a time in hot fat. Remove when golden brown.

Serves 6.   *   *   *

Additional recipes for onions will be found under Appetizers, Pickles and Relishes, Salads, and Soups.

OYSTER PLANT (*see* page 153).

Parsley

THIS dark-green, crisp, deeply frilled vegetable is too rich in flavor and vitamins to be carelessly pushed aside when used as a garnish. Train yourself to eat it. The flavor is pungent.

Be sure that the parsley is well washed and drained before being used or stored in the vegetable crisper in the refrigerator.

Just because one small clump or large sprig is effective in garnishing, do not think a whole hedge of parsley will be just that much more so. Try putting one small clump at one part of the platter; then put a much larger bunch at another, perhaps opposite, spot. You will find it effective.

BUYING GUIDE: See Greens (page 99).

* * *

See Appetizers, Salads, and Soups.

Parsnips

Parsnips are one of the few vegetables that have a naturally sweetish flavor. Actually the sweetness is developed as the vegetables stay underground during a spell of really cold weather.

Low-income North European families used to make parsnips their main food. Later, of course, potatoes superseded parsnips. Parsnips lend themselves to several dishes. Cooked in boiling salted water, they can then be sautéed, or mashed and made into patties or fritters.

Buying Guide: Smooth, firm, and well shaped; small to medium size. Flabby, shriveled roots usually indicate pithiness. Large coarse roots usually have woody cores. Watch for indications of decay.

Basic Rule for Cooking Parsnips

Wash parsnips and scrape skin. If skin seems tough, pare them. Cook whole, or cut into lengthwise quarters or thick slices. Put the parsnips in rapidly boiling salted water. Cook until tender but not mushy.

MASHED PARSNIPS

Mash cooked parsnips. Season with salt, pepper. Add a generous amount of butter.

PARSNIP PATTIES

Mash and season parsnips. When cold, shape into flat cakes. (The mashed parsnips should not be watery.)

Flour cakes lightly. Sauté in hot bacon fat. Serve with crisp bacon.

CANDIED PARSNIPS

12 parsnips	1/3 cup orange juice
1 teaspoon salt	1 tablespoon grated orange
1/3 cup maple sirup	rind
½ cup butter or margarine	

Parboil parsnips. Drain. Cut in thick lengthwise slices. Place in shallow baking dish. Sprinkle lightly with salt. Combine sirup and orange juice and rind. Pour over the parsnips. Dot with butter. Bake in a 375-degree oven until liquids are absorbed.

Serves 4 to 6.

GLAZED PARSNIPS

6 parsnips	3 tablespoons butter
2 teaspoons salt	¼ cup brown sugar
1 tablespoon flour	¼ teaspoon cinnamon

Slice parsnips ⅓ inch thick, cover with water, and boil until tender. Drain.

Sprinkle with salt, dredge with flour, and brown in butter. Arrange in baking dish. Sprinkle with brown sugar and cinnamon. Bake at 325 degrees for 15 to 20 minutes, or until sugar melts and parsnips are heated.

Serves 6.

POTPIE OF PARSNIPS

¼ pound bacon
1 medium-sized onion
2 cups sliced raw parsnips

2 cups diced potatoes
Salt and pepper
Garnish

Cut bacon in small pieces and pan-fry in hot pan with onion until onion is brown. Add parsnips and potatoes. Brown lightly.

Transfer to deep kettle and pour in enough stock or water barely to cover. Allow to simmer until the vegetables are cooked.

Drain and place on hot platter. Boil down the liquid to less than a pint. Season and pour around the vegetables.

Garnish with a border of dumplings, green beans, or Lima beans.

Serves 6.

PARSNIPS WITH BACON

6 parsnips
2 cups water
½ teaspoon salt

¼ cup grated cheese
3 tablespoons bread crumbs
½ to 1 cup thin cream

2 slices bacon

Pare parsnips and boil in salted water until tender. Slice lengthwise and arrange in greased baking dish in alternate layers with cheese and bread crumbs.

Pour cream over mixture. Cut up bacon and sprinkle over top. Bake at 400 degrees 30 to 35 minutes.

Serves 6.

*   *   *

Additional recipes for parsnips will be found under Soups, How To Freeze Vegetables, and Home Canning of Vegetables.

Green Peas

LONDONERS used to hear this call:

> *Green peas, I say; green peas, I say, here:*
> *Have 'em at your own price; here; here;*
> *Sixpence a peck these peas are sold;*
> *Fresh and green, and far from old.*

That call gives one of the tests for peas: They must be young and tender. Cooked in a small amount of salted water and served with nothing but butter or heavy cream, they are an epicure's idea of the perfect vegetable.

Some cooks put a pinch of sugar in the cooking water. Others add a sprig or two of mint.

Many years ago, French chefs wrapped raw peas in lettuce leaves and put them in a saucepan with a little butter. The saucepan was then lightly covered and set over a low fire.

[124]

That method is being revived today. It brings out an excellent flavor.

Some varieties of peas are cooked and eaten pods and all. This brings to mind Lydgate's couplet:

> Were women as little as they are good
> A peascod would make them a gown and a hood.

Buying Guide: Well-filled bright pods, velvety to the touch. Immature pods are flat, dark green in color, may have wilted appearance. Yellowish and swollen pod indicates overmaturity.

Basic Rule for Cooking Fresh Peas

When peas are young and fresh and newly arrived in the market, they should be served often. Like asparagus, their advent used to be seasonal and hailed with enthusiasm. Green peas are good at any time, but they used to taste like ambrosia when they made their first appearance in early summer.

When peas are young and have been gathered a short time before they are shelled and cooked, they need nothing but butter, or a little cream, to make them superlatively good.

No wonder New Englanders celebrate the Fourth of July with boiled fresh salmon, new buttered potatoes, and fresh peas. That's a feast fit for the gods.

Shell peas. Discard immature ones, as well as those that feel hard as a rock. These are too old to be changed by cooking into sweet, tender morsels. Rinse the shelled peas to remove bits of pod or leaf.

Drop into a small amount of rapidly boiling salted water. Cook until peas are tender, still fresh green, and not mushy.

Watch time when using pressure saucepan. The cooking time, once the pressure is at the required point, is practically less than nothing. Reduce pressure quickly.

GREEN PEAS WITH BUTTER

Dress hot cooked peas with butter. Chopped mint may be added.

GREEN PEAS IN CREAM

Pour a small amount of cream over drained cooked peas. You may want to add a smidgin of sugar.

PEAS LORRAINE

2 pounds peas	1 teaspoon sugar
3 tablespoons butter	½ teaspoon salt
½ cup water	¼ teaspoon pepper
2 tablespoons minced onion	Nutmeg
1 tablespoon chopped parsley	4 to 6 lettuce leaves
½ cup cream	

Heat butter and water; add peas, shelled, onion, parsley, sugar, and seasonings. Cover and cook until peas are almost tender.

Add finely shredded lettuce. Cook 5 minutes longer.

Add cream.

Serves 6.

FRENCH PEAS

2 cups fresh peas	¼ cup butter
½ head lettuce	2 teaspoons sugar
1 onion	½ teaspoon salt

Sliver lettuce and cut onion in thin slices. Put peas, onion, and lettuce in saucepan, add butter and seasonings. Cook over medium heat, stirring frequently, until peas are tender, 15 to 20 minutes.

Serves 4.

* * *

Additional recipes for peas will be found under Salads, Soups, How To Freeze Vegetables, and Home Canning of Vegetables.

Peppers

Green, red, or yellow; blunt-nosed or sharp-pointed; sweet or hot; large or tiny—there is the story of peppers grown in gardens and sold in stores.

These vegetables are not the source of the black, red, and white pepper used on the table, but they can seem just as hot.

Christopher Columbus was commissioned by Queen Isabella of Spain to find a new and quick sailing route to the Indies, home of spices which sold for fabulous prices. He failed, but did "discover" America.

He found plants bearing glossy green globes growing on the land. When eaten, they filled the mouth with something as hot as liquid fire. To Columbus, who was not a botanist, this plant was definitely the source of pepper. He so named it. We have kept the name even though we know his deduction was wrong.

A mild, sweet pepper is called "pimiento"; the hot one is called "chili" (used in chili con carne). A Hungarian sweet red pepper is the source of paprika. The tiny red pepper, scarcely an inch in length, is used in making tabasco sauce.

None of these peppers is used in making table pepper.

BUYING GUIDE: Even shape, firm and thick-fleshed, uniform and glossy in color. Beware of pale color, sunken blisterlike spots, flabby flesh.

Basic Rule for Preparing Green Peppers

Green peppers look cool but beware! The seeds and white pithy sections inside the pepper contain a substance which is intensely irritating to the skin. It causes excruciating pain when it comes in contact with eyes and lips.

Cut off top or stem end. With a knife or spoon, scrape out seeds and white pith. Be careful not to touch lips or eyes during this process.

Green peppers are used raw in many ways. Rings may be cut through which bundles of green beans or asparagus stalks are inserted.

Rings may top a salad in a desired design.

Slender strips are ornamental and are used frequently.

Finely chopped raw green pepper may be added to cabbage slaw or cottage cheese. (This is not recommended, since some people cannot eat raw green peppers.)

Green peppers may be cut into pieces and put in soups, stews, meat dishes, etc., that will be cooked before being served.

Green peppers, either cut into lengthwise halves or left standing upright, may be filled with mixtures and then baked. Many people parboil the peppers before using them in this fashion. If stuffed peppers are set upright in muffin-pan wells or in custard cups, they are less likely to lose their shape as they cook.

STUFFED GREEN PEPPERS

Well-seasoned uncooked ground beef, tomato pulp, cooked rice, and seasonings make a good stuffing. Cooking time 40 minutes, temperature 350 degrees.

Sausage meat, finely crumbled potato chips, and cooked macaroni may be combined as a stuffing. Cooking time and temperature the same. The filling used for mushroom caps on page 110 may be used.

In every case, put finely crumbled potato chips, or corn-flakes, or buttered freshly crumbed bread over top.

Baked stuffed peppers may be served with tomato sauce, or with canned mushroom soup which has been diluted and heated.

*   *   *

Additional recipes for peppers will be found under Appetizers, Pickles and Relishes, Salads, and Sandwiches.

PIE PLANT (*see* Rhubarb, page 147).

Potatoes

"THE WORLD'S Number One Vegetable" is the title worn proudly by the potato. Eaten day in and day out, it offers bulk, mineral salts, vitamins, and bland flavor.

Ireland is not the home of the Irish potato, oddly enough. Its native habitat is somewhere in South America, near Peru, Bolivia, and Ecuador.

Potatoes are one of the few vegetables that can be used in one form or another for every dinner course from soup to dessert.

BUYING GUIDE: Clean, firm, and smooth; shallow eyes evenly shaped. Potatoes should not show fleshy sprouts, watery appearance, or sponginess. Avoid green color; this is sunburn and it gives a bitter flavor.

Basic Rule for Cooking Potatoes

"Good plain cooks" are frequently overrated. They are likely to serve soggy boiled potatoes and steak fried like leather. A really good cook boils potatoes and serves them hot, mealy, and well flavored. She selects the right potato for the job. A mealy potato such as has been developed in Idaho and in Maine is meant for baking, not for boiling.

Certain kinds of potatoes become waxy when boiled and beaten. The more they are beaten the smoother and more slippery they are. Good cooking could not have prevented that condition, but selecting the right potato would have.

The Scandinavian countries grow potatoes that have a delicious flavor and a mealy texture when boiled. That is one reason why boiled potatoes are so popular over there.

Select the right kind of potatoes for the kind of cooking you plan.

Raw potatoes can be boiled, baked, fried in deep fat. In each case the potato is raw to start with.

Baking potatoes may be identified by shape. They should be flattish with rounded ends. The skin should be thin, slightly rough, and russet tan in color.

BOILED POTATOES

Wash potatoes. Cook with skins or jackets on. Cook in rapidly boiling salted water. As soon as the potatoes are done, remove the skins. Put the potatoes back in the dry saucepan and shake it over a low fire for a minute or two. This dries the potato, preventing sogginess.

Boiled potatoes may be dressed with melted butter. Freshly ground salt and pepper, chopped chives, or parsley are good additions.

RICED POTATOES

Boil potatoes. After shaking dry in the pan, put them through a sieve or ricer. Do not smooth them down, but serve them fluffy and piled high in a hot serving dish.

MASHED POTATOES

Boil and rice hot potatoes. Add hot milk in which butter has been melted (a minimum of 2 tablespoons milk and 1 teaspoon butter per potato). Beat with a large fork, a slotted spoon, or use an electric mixer to whip the mass to something looking like a fleecy cloud. Do this quickly, so the potatoes will not get lukewarm.

Pile the potatoes into a serving dish. Make a depression in center of the potatoes and put in a large piece of butter. This melts and looks like a pool of molten gold. Add a little paprika if desired.

CREAMED POTATOES

Boiled potatoes which have been diced and combined with a thin cream sauce are improved by a sprinkling of chopped chives or parsley.

Many cooks prefer diced cold *baked* potatoes for creaming. In this case, top milk or cream is poured on the potatoes. They are cooked over slow heat until the cream is almost all absorbed.

BAKED POTATOES

Select large potatoes of uniform size. Wash. Some cooks rub skins with butter or cooking oil. This is supposed to make the skin more crisp and better tasting. Put potatoes in 350-degree oven. Allow approximately an hour for baking. Test for doneness by squeezing hot potato gently in palm protected by pot holder. If the potato is soft it is done and should be pricked to allow steam to escape. Also, it should be served at once.

POPPED POTATOES

Bake large potatoes. When done, make two short cuts at right angles to each other on top of potato. Squeeze gently.

The mealy, steaming pulp pops up through the opening. Put on a lump of butter. Serve at once.

BAKED POTATOES WITH SAUSAGE

Use apple corer to make hole lengthwise through middle of potato. Insert small sausage link. Plug ends of holes with potato. Bake, keeping the potatoes on baking sheet to catch the drip from cooking sausage.

POTATO BALLS

Cut small balls out of raw potatoes. Use French ball cutter. (Unused framework of potatoes may be cooked, riced, mashed, and shaped into flat cakes.) Melt butter. Roll raw balls into butter until they are coated on all sides. Salt lightly.

Place balls in shallow baking dish which can be covered. Set dish in 375-degree oven. Shake the dish occasionally to prevent balls from sticking to bottom. Bake until balls are soft and a golden brown. Uncover during last part of cooking.

VARIATION: Balls may be rolled in beef drippings in place of butter.

POTATO CAKES

Shape freshly mashed potatoes or warm, leftover mashed potatoes into flat cakes. Chill. Roll lightly in seasoned flour.

Panfry in small amount of fat in heavy frying pan. Turn to brown both sides.

LATE COMERS' MASHED POTATOES

If you are having mashed potatoes and fear the guests may be late, use this method, which keeps potatoes hot but prevents that standing-around flavor. Add more milk than usual to potatoes when mashing them. Spread them in a heavy oven-glass baking pan. Pour top milk over them. Add a few dots of butter. Set the pan, uncovered, in a 350-degree oven. The top becomes a beautiful golden brown and the potatoes stay hot and absorb the extra moisture.

POTATO CROQUETTES

Shape mashed potatoes into balls, cylinders, or cones. Do this while they are still pliable, but not too hot to handle.

Chill them well. Roll in flour, or potato flour.

Put a few at a time in a frying basket immersed in deep fat heated to 360 degrees. Remove when golden brown.

STUFFED BAKED POTATO COMBINATIONS

Freshly baked potatoes may be cut in halves lengthwise. The potato pulp is scooped out, mashed, and made fluffy before being put back into the potato shells. The mashed potato may be changed in flavor by adding a few grains of nutmeg, a little thyme or marjoram.

Leftover cooked string beans may be folded into the fluffy mashed potato. So may well-cooked sausage meat or finely chopped bacon. Any one of these mixtures is improved by the addition of an egg yolk, plenty of butter, and a little milk.

Brown the refilled potato halves in the oven or under the broiler flame.

DUCHESS POTATOES

To 3 cups of hot mashed potatoes add 2 lightly beaten egg yolks. Beat well.

Put mixture in pastry bag. Force the mashed potato through the rose tube and through the flat, serrated-edge ribbon tube to make potato roses and potato borders. These may be formed directly onto a plank holding steak or fish. The mixture is put on during the last 15 minutes of cooking of steak or fish. The edges of the roses and ribbon become a golden brown.

LEMON PARSLEY POTATOES

1½ quarts potatoes   5 teaspoons lemon juice
2 tablespoons butter   1 tablespoon parsley

Pare and cube potatoes and boil them in salted water. When tender, remove from fire and drain. Shake over heat to let steam escape.

Add butter and lemon juice. Shake gently so that each cube will be flavored. Sprinkle with chopped parsley.

Serves 6.

KOLCANNON

2 pounds potatoes   ¼ cup thick cream
2 pounds cabbage   1 tablespoon salt
½ cup butter   1 teaspoon pepper

Boil potatoes with skins on. Peel. Put through ricer.

Chop and boil cabbage. Combine with potatoes. Add butter and cream. Season. Stir over fire until hot and serve in the shape of a mound or cake.

Serves 6.

POTATOES REGAL

10 potatoes   1/16 teaspoon pepper
½ cup grated cheese   3 eggs
1 teaspoon salt   1 cup milk

Wash and pare potatoes and slice about ⅛ inch thick. Put layer in baking dish; sprinkle with cheese and seasonings. Repeat.

Beat eggs slightly. Add milk. Pour over mixture in casserole. Bake at 375 degrees for 45 minutes.

Serves 6.

HUNGARIAN STYLE POTATOES

6 medium potatoes   Salt
2 tablespoons butter   1½ teaspoons caraway seeds

Boil potatoes in their jackets. Peel while hot.

Heat butter in heavy frying pan. Add potatoes. Place over low heat. Shake from time to time. Cook until the potatoes acquire a delicate brown crust.

Drain and sprinkle with salt and caraway seeds.

Hungarian-style potatoes are especially fine with a pot roast or a roast leg of lamb.

Serves 6.

SCALLOPED POTATOES

9 potatoes, medium-sized   1 teaspoon salt
3 tablespoons flour   Freshly ground pepper
6 to 8 tablespoons butter or   3 cups milk
   margarine   Bacon strips (optional)

Wash and pare potatoes and cut them in ¼-inch-thick slices.

Place a layer of potatoes in bottom of baking dish. Put approximately ½ of the flour, butter, salt, and pepper over the layer of potatoes. Add second layer of potatoes and remaining flour, butter, salt, and pepper. Add third or top layer. Pour milk into casserole, bringing the milk just up to the top layer of potatoes.

Cover the casserole and set in an oven preheated to 350 degrees. Remove the cover when the mixture begins to bubble and looks as though it would run over.

Strips of bacon may be put on top when the cover is removed.

NOTE: Sometimes scalloped potatoes have a curdled appearance. This is due to the action of the acid (in the potatoes) and the salt on the milk. This can be obviated by using the same proportions of flour, butter, and milk as given in above recipe, making a thin cream sauce and pouring it over the sliced raw potatoes in the casserole.

NOTE: If the sauce persists in running over the sides of the casserole, place a pan of water under the casserole to catch the sauce.

Serves 6.

PERSILLADE POTATOES

1½ pounds small new
   potatoes
4 tablespoons butter

¼ cup chopped parsley
2 tablespoons lemon juice
Salt

Boil potatoes in salted water. Remove skins.

Melt butter and add parsley, lemon juice, and salt. Mix and pour over hot boiled potatoes.

Serves 6.

RANCH POTATOES

¼ cup margarine
5 medium-sized potatoes,
   peeled and sliced thin
2 small onions, peeled and
   sliced thin

½ teaspoon salt
¼ teaspoon celery seed
Freshly ground black pepper

Melt margarine over medium heat. When margarine is hot, add potatoes, onions, and seasonings. Cover and cook for about 25 minutes over medium heat. Turn potatoes occasionally with a large spatula. Potatoes should be golden brown and tender when done.

Serves 6.

POTATOES WITH CHEESE SAUCE

2 tablespoons butter
2 tablespoons flour
1 cup milk
½ teaspoon salt

⅛ teaspoon pepper
1 cup Cheddar cheese
1 teaspoon lemon juice
2 cups diced potatoes

Melt butter. Add flour. Cook until bubbling. Add milk. Stir until thickened and smooth. Season well. Add cheese. Stir until cheese is melted. Add lemon juice.

Combine with cooked potatoes in baking dish. Bake at 350 degrees until mixture is bubbling.

Serves 6.

LUNCHEON POTATOES

1 small onion
½ pound mushrooms
4 tablespoons butter
3 tablespoons flour
2 cups milk

1 teaspoon salt
¼ teaspoon pepper
3 cups cooked potatoes, sliced
6 hard-cooked eggs, sliced
Pimiento

Chop onion, slice mushrooms, and sauté in butter. Add flour, stirring well. Add milk. Stir until mixture thickens.

Place alternate layers of sliced potatoes and eggs in casserole. Pour the sauce over the mixture. Add bits of pimiento, if desired.

Bake in a 375-degree oven until sauce is bubbling (approximately ½ hour).

Serves 6.

CREAMED POTATOES AND EGGS

½ green pepper, diced
1 small onion, sliced
2 tablespoons fat
1 tablespoon flour
1 can mushroom soup

1 soup can milk
Salt and pepper
Paprika
4 potatoes
6 eggs, hard-cooked

Sauté green pepper and onion in fat. Add flour, mix well. Add soup and milk. Cook until thickened, stirring to keep smooth. Season.

Add cooked and diced potatoes and hard-cooked eggs, cut into quarters.

Reheat. Serve with a green vegetable.
Serves 6.

CHANTILLY POTATOES WITH HAM

2 cups riced potatoes
¼ cup hot milk
2 tablespoons butter
½ cup cooked ham
½ cup whipping cream
1 cup Cheddar cheese
Salt and pepper
Paprika

Beat the potatoes, milk, and butter until fluffy.

Pile on a glass baking dish. Sprinkle with the finely chopped ham.

Whip the cream. Grate and add the cheese, with seasonings to taste.

Spread this over the ham and potatoes and bake in a hot oven, 450 degrees, 10 to 15 minutes.
Serves 6.

POTATOES IN CREAM

4 cups diced potatoes
2 cups thin cream
3 tablespoons butter
Salt and pepper

Pare and boil potatoes. Cut in small dice, about ¼ inch in size.

Put in upper part of double boiler. Add cream, butter, and seasonings.

Let potatoes stay over simmering hot water in lower part of double boiler until the cream has been absorbed. This takes about 2 hours.
Serves 6.

POTATO PANCAKES

2 cups grated raw potatoes   ⅛ teaspoon baking powder
2 beaten eggs   1 tablespoon flour
1 teaspoon salt   1 tablespoon grated onion
            Pinch of thyme

Drain the potatoes well and immediately blend with the eggs and other ingredients.

Drop batter by spoonfuls onto a hot well-greased griddle. Brown deeply on each side and serve hot.

Serves 6.

KARTOFFEL KLOESE

8 potatoes   Paprika
¾ cup melted shortening   Nutmeg
4 slices dry bread, finely cubed   ¼ teaspoon thyme (optional)
Salt   3 eggs, separated
Pepper   Flour

Boil potatoes. When cold, put through ricer.

Melt shortening in frying pan. When hot, brown cubed bread to a golden brown. Add to potatoes.

Add salt, pepper, paprika, nutmeg, and thyme.

Add egg yolks. Sift flour over mixture to make it of a consistency to knead.

Knead thoroughly and add stiffly beaten egg whites. Form in balls. Try one in boiling salted water to make sure consistency is right. Boil in salted water about 10 minutes.

Brown. Keep warm.

Serves 6.

SWEET CREAM POTATOES

6 potatoes   3 tablespoons butter
2 cups thin cream   Salt and pepper

Boil and dice potatoes and place in a heavy skillet. Add the cream and butter and season. Cook over low heat, stirring frequently until thick, about 15 minutes.

Serves 6.

POTATO LEMON CUSTARD PIE

1 medium-sized potato
2 tablespoons butter
¾ cup sugar
½ teaspoon salt

2 eggs, separated
½ cup milk
½ lemon, juice and grated rind

Cook potato in boiling salted water. Mash. Add butter, sugar, and salt. When cool, add egg yolks, milk, and lemon juice and rind.

Fold in stiffly beaten egg whites.

Pour into unbaked pie shell and bake at 400 degrees for 35 minutes, or until knife blade inserted in center of filling comes out clean.

Serves 6.

*   *   *

Additional recipes for potatoes will be found under Salads and Soups.

Pumpkin

WHEN the frost is on the "punkin" goblins and witches ride high in the sky. Halloween is at hand. Pumpkin pie and Halloween go together as naturally as do pumpkin lanterns and black cats.

Crookneck pumpkin are popular down South, but most of us think of them as orange globes that polka-dot the autumn fields or add color to roadside stands in the early autumn. Pumpkins, like squash, mold and spoil quickly once they are cut open. Actually, much of the "pumpkin" used in pie is orange-fleshed squash.

BUYING GUIDE: Pumpkins should have fairly firm rinds and be bright orange in color, should be heavy for size and free from blemishes. The smaller pumpkin should contain a good proportion of flesh to size and have more tender flesh than large ones.

Basic Rule for Cooking Pumpkin

Halloween "punkin" lanterns become a food waste unless the pumpkin is cooked after the special occasion. This cooking must be done within a day or two after the pumpkin has been cut open. Almost before your eyes the inside molds and shows a feathery black that spells the end of that pumpkin.

Cut pumpkin into pieces. Wash and pare the pieces.

Since pumpkin is watery, it is best to steam or cook the pieces in a pressure saucepan.

Mash the cooked pumpkin.

Use the pumpkin purée within a day or two. Canning and processing is the only way in which cooked pumpkin will keep without spoiling for any length of time.

Use pumpkin purée in pumpkin pie. Pumpkin cake, a spicy one, is good, but uses only a small amount of pumpkin purée.

Pumpkin chips, a sort of rich, sweet preserve, is popular in some homes. But it needs the addition of lemon and ginger root to offset the cloying sweetness of preserved pumpkin.

RICH PUMPKIN PIE

Unbaked pie crust
¾ teaspoon cinnamon
¾ teaspoon nutmeg
⅜ teaspoon ginger
⅛ teaspoon cloves
¾ teaspoon salt
¾ cup sugar
2 cups pumpkin purée
2 cups cream
3 eggs, separated

Line pie plate with pastry. Set in refrigerator until ready to be filled.

Add the spices and salt to the sugar. Add to the strained, stewed pumpkin.

Add the cream. Stir until blended.

Beat egg whites. Add yolks. Combine eggs with first mixture.

Pour into pie crust and bake for 10 minutes in a 450-degree oven. Reduce heat to 350 degrees and bake for 40 minutes, or until an inserted knife blade comes out clean.

NOTE: Two cups cooked carrot purée may be substituted for the pumpkin. The resulting texture is the same, the flavor is similar, and the nutrients are even greater.

Serves 6.

INEXPENSIVE PUMPKIN PIE

Unbaked pie crust
¾ teaspoon cinnamon
¾ teaspoon nutmeg
⅜ teaspoon ginger
¾ teaspoon salt

1 1/3 cups sweetened
  condensed milk
1 cup water
2 cups pumpkin purée
3 eggs, separated

Line pie plate with pastry. Set in refrigerator until ready to be filled.

Follow the directions for Rich Pumpkin Pie filling (*see* page 143), noting that the sweetened condensed milk and water are substituted for cream and sugar.

Serves 6.

Radishes

A RADISH is a rather rank-growing vegetable that matures quickly. This may explain its popularity with young gardeners, but offers no real reason for the radish's high valuation by the Greeks, who reproduced radishes in solid gold. A peppery, biting quality gives radishes a place on a relish tray. Rose, white, and black radishes may be found in some markets. The black ones are a winter variety and may be stored like turnips.

Orientals use large radishes for a popular pickled dish. Occasionally radishes are boiled in salted water and eaten hot with butter and salt.

Radishes are usually eaten raw as a relish or used raw as a garnish. Radish roses are made by making short, horizontal cuts or gashes at intervals around the sides of round radishes. After immersion in ice water, the slits open, giving the effect of petals.

BUYING GUIDE: Smooth, clear-colored, uniform size, solid, fresh green tops, small-leaved, clean. Spongy, large, yellow-leaved, dull-colored, radishes are usually strong in flavor; flesh may be woody.

RADISHES WITH HOLLANDAISE SAUCE AND CHIVES

3 cups radishes
1 cup Hollandaise sauce
¼ cup chopped chives

Cook unpeeled radishes in boiling salted water. Drain. Dress with sauce and chives.

Rhubarb

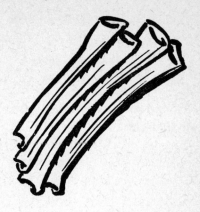

"PIEPLANT" is a popular name for rhubarb and deservedly so! What tastes better than fresh rhubarb pie on a day in spring?

The mushy stem end and the leaves (which contain a poisonous ingredient) are discarded. Tender stalks are cut, skin and all, into short lengths. Cooked rhubarb has a beautiful rosy color, especially if one of the bright-red varieties is used. Home-grown rhubarb which stays in the garden too long develops a tough skin, a green color, and a definitely stringy stalk.

BUYING GUIDE: Straight, firm, fairly thick stalks; brilliant red color. Old rhubarb is pithy, tough, and stringy, and usually dull in color.

Basic Rule for Cooking Rhubarb

Cooking is not too kind to rhubarb. What starts out as a rosy-pink, almost brittle stalk ends up as a pale-pink shapeless sauce. But we eat rhubarb primarily for its flavor. Welcome indeed is the sweet, tart sauce or pie filling.

Grown-under-glass rhubarb is brighter in color, less stringy, and more tender-skinned than the home-grown variety. In using the home-grown stalks, avoid the ones that are dark green, stringy, and tough. They are way past their prime.

Wash stalks. Discard the leafy part. Cut off the pithy base. Skin may be left on or taken off, depending on its tenderness. Cut stalk into short lengths.

Pieces of rhubarb may be cooked in a small amount of water in a saucepan. Sweeten to taste.

Hotels and restaurants serve a rhubarb sauce consisting of a sirup and inch pieces of pink or "strawberry" rhubarb. The small pieces have been poached or cooked for a few minutes in the sirup. The result is attractive, but the sauce is quite tasteless.

RHUBARB AND BANANAS

Cook rhubarb as in baked rhubarb sauce recipe (*see* page 149). Slice 2 bananas into individual sauce dishes. Put rhubarb sauce over the bananas. Chill thoroughly and serve.

RHUBARB WHIP

3 egg whites	1/16 teaspoon salt
3 tablespoons powdered sugar	1 teaspoon lemon juice
1½ cups rhubarb sauce	

Whip egg whites until they stand in peaks. Beat in powdered sugar, salt, and lemon juice. Fold in the rhubarb sauce.

Serve in sherbet glasses. Sprinkle with nut meats, or serve with custard sauce.

Serves 6.

BAKED RHUBARB SAUCE

Cut rhubarb stalks into small pieces. Mix with half as much sugar as there is rhubarb. Let stand for 2 hours. Put in tightly covered casserole and bake in oven at 325 degrees, for about 45 minutes. Remove cover during the latter part of baking.

This sauce is rich in flavor. It is not watery or dingy in color, as a stewed rhubarb sauce is likely to be.

A few pieces of candied ginger add good flavor.

Baked rhubarb sauce may be served with blanc mange, vanilla pudding, or cottage pudding.

RHUBARB CUSTARD PIE

Unbaked pie crust
1 cup sugar
3 tablespoons flour

⅛ teaspoon salt
2 eggs
3 cups rhubarb cut in ½-inch pieces

Line pie plate with pastry. Set in refrigerator until ready to be filled.

Combine sugar, 2 tablespoons flour, and salt. Add slightly beaten eggs.

Add rhubarb. Sprinkle 1 tablespoon flour over bottom crust. Fill crust with rhubarb mixture. Put on lattice top.

Bake in an oven preheated to 450 degrees for 10 minutes. Reduce the heat to 350 degrees and continue baking for 30 minutes more.

Serves 6.

FRESH RHUBARB PIE

Unbaked pie crust
3 to 4 cups pink rhubarb
1 cup sugar

3 tablespoons flour
⅛ teaspoon salt
1/16 teaspoon cinnamon

Line pie plate with pastry. Set in refrigerator until ready to be filled.

Wash stalks of rhubarb. Cut off stem and pithy end. Leave skin on. Cut in ½-inch pieces.

Mix sugar, flour, salt, and cinnamon. Add to rhubarb.

Pour into pie crust. Put on top crust.

Bake in an oven preheated to 450 degrees for 10 minutes. Reduce the heat to 350 degrees and continue baking for 20 to 30 minutes longer.

Serves 6.

Rutabagas

Cᴀʟʟ them "yellow turnips" or "Swedes," if you will, but they still are rutabagas. The ocher-colored solid flesh is covered with a skin of the same shade which becomes purplish near the stem end. Rutabagas are cabbage-turnip hybrids, having characteristics of both vegetables. They were the first root-stock vegetable to be waxed on the surface to increase their keeping qualities. Wax and skins are removed before cooking.

Bᴜʏɪɴɢ Gᴜɪᴅᴇ: Roots solid and heavy for size; smooth skin; should be treated with edible wax for keeping quality.

Basic Rule for Cooking Rutabagas

The rutabaga is a forthright vegetable. The inside is the same color as the outside. The flavor is earthy, lacking the pungency of the turnip.

Rutabagas may be washed, but the wax or paraffin has been put over a clean surface by the grower. Washing is not necessary, really.

Cut rutabaga in slices, chunks, or fair-sized pieces. Pare the pieces. They are easy to hold while paring off the outer skin. A whole rutabaga is too large to handle comfortably. Thick slices may be cut into dice, if preferred.

Steam or cook in pressure saucepan, or in boiling salted water. Drain.

MASHED RUTABAGA WITH CARROTS

1 rutabaga   1/3 cup brown sugar
8 carrots   Salt and pepper
2 tablespoons butter   Nutmeg
                 ¼ cup chopped parsley

Pare and cube rutabaga. Scrape carrots. Cook rutabaga and carrots in boiling salted water. Mash.

Add remaining ingredients and serve hot.

Serves 6.

Salsify or Oyster Plant

BECAUSE salsify has a flavor reminiscent of oysters, it is called "oyster plant"; because the tuft of leaves which extend above the earth resemble the tuft on a goat's chin, the vegetable is often called "goat's beard." None of the names increases the popularity of this vegetable. It may be that its dark appearance when cooked is a deterrent. But it's a vegetable that could well be used more frequently.

BUYING GUIDE: Firm, well-shaped root; medium size. Flabby, shriveled roots are fibrous or pithy; large, coarse roots have woody cores. Decay appears in form of gray mold.

Basic Rule for Cooking Salsify

Salsify is one of the lesser-used vegetables. The flavor is faintly reminiscent of an oyster, but the color of the cooked vegetable is its least attractive quality.

[153]

Wash roots. Pare them. Put pared roots into slightly acidulated water. This helps to prevent too much darkening of salsify.

Cut roots into inch lengths. Cook in boiling salted water. Dress with melted butter.

Spinach

Spinach has had its up and downs, nutritionally speaking, within the past thirty-some years. But now it is accepted for its great contribution to the vitamin needs of the human body.

During the time when spinach was considered indispensable, nutritionally, it became necessary for women to devise ways of preparing spinach to make it more generally acceptable. Families refuse to eat overcooked, sodden, unappetizing vegetables, no matter how "good for them."

Today's cooked spinach may have good looks and good flavor in addition to good nutritional value.

Buying Guide: Dark, well-mottled; large leaves; clean, free from grit. Decay in form of soft slimy rot. Avoid coarse leaf and tough and woody stems. Yellowing spinach should be examined carefully.

Methods of cooking spinach are given under Greens, page 99.

* * *

SPINACH TIMBALES

2 cups cooked spinach	1/16 teaspoon pepper
2 cups milk	4 eggs
1½ cups crumbed bread	1 tablespoon grated onion
4 tablespoons butter	1 tablespoon lemon juice
1 teaspoon salt	2 cups cheese sauce (page 223)

Chop and drain cooked spinach. Heat milk. Add bread crumbs, beaten eggs, and all other ingredients. Mix well.

Pour into oiled molds or custard cups. Set in pan containing hot water.

Bake in moderate oven, 350 degrees, for 40 to 50 minutes, or until knife comes out clean when inserted in center.

Unmold. Surround with sautéed mushrooms on tomato slices. Pour cheese sauce over all.

Serves 6.

SPINACH RING WITH CREAMED MUSHROOMS

2 pounds fresh spinach	1 tablespoon melted butter
5 egg yolks	Salt and pepper
¼ cup cream	Creamed mushrooms (page 110)

Cook spinach about ten minutes in a small amount of boiling water. Chop fine, or press through a coarse sieve after the spinach has been well drained.

Mix the beaten egg yolks with cream and melted butter, salt, and pepper. Add spinach.

Press this mixture into a well-greased ring mold, cover top with waxed paper, and set in pan of hot water to steam in the oven until firm, about 45 minutes, at 350 degrees.

Unmold on a hot platter and fill the center with creamed mushrooms.

Serves 6.

SPINACH SUPREME

½ pound Cheddar cheese
1/3 cup milk
2½ cups cooked spinach

Salt and pepper
1½ cups freshly crumbed bread
3 strips bacon

Melt cheese in top of double boiler. Add the milk gradually, stirring constantly until the sauce is smooth.

Drain spinach well and add to the cheese mixture, with seasonings to taste.

Place in a casserole and cover with soft bread crumbs. Lay on bacon strips, cut in half.

Bake in moderate oven, 350 degrees, for 30 minutes.

Serves 6.

SPINACH PIE

1 pound spinach, raw
6 raw potatoes
3 eggs

1 onion
4 tablespoons melted butter
1 teaspoon salt
1/16 teaspoon pepper

Chop raw spinach very fine.

Grate potatoes and add the beaten eggs to avoid discoloration. Grate onion into mixture. Add melted butter and seasonings.

Place half potato mixture in baking dish, pack in spinach, cover with rest of potato mixture. Bake at 350 degrees for about 30 minutes.

Serves 6.   *   *   *

Additional recipes for spinach will be found under Salads and Soups.

Squash

The American Indians had a name for it: "*askutasquash.*"
Actually, the last syllable in that long name is descriptive of
what the vegetable comes to once it is cooked. It's squashed
all right, but good! Summer squash take many shapes and
sizes, but basically they all have a thin tender skin, a palish
yellow or green pulp, and seeds that are tender enough to be
eaten unless the squash is overripe.

Some of the names indicate the shapes. There's patty-pan
squash (cymling in the South), crookneck squash (sometimes
straight), vegetable marrow (popular in England), cocozelle,
and zucchini (well known in Italy and gaining in acceptance
here). Butternut squash is smooth-skinned, dull yellow,
orange-fleshed. Summer squashes are rather bland in flavor.
Add flavor by using flavorful stuffings or sauces.

Winter squashes are hard-shelled and deep-yellow or orange-fleshed, with mature seeds enmeshed in a fibrous substance. The shell may be dark green (Hubbard squash) or slaty blue (blue Hubbard). The surface is somewhat rough and warty. Acorn or nutmeg squashes are miniature ones, just large enough to serve two people when halved and cooked. The skin is dark green and smooth but deeply furrowed. These squash have good keeping qualities as long as they are left whole; once opened, the flesh molds and spoils within a few days.

BUYING GUIDE: Small to medium size, free from blemishes, fairly heavy for size.

Basic Rule for Cooking Squash

Squash may be hard-shelled or soft-shelled, smooth-skinned or ridged or warty. Colors vary from pale green to deep bottle green and from pale yellow to brilliant orange.

The most recent comer to make a strong bid for popularity is butternut squash. It is rather hard-shelled, almost pastel pumpkin in color. Its flesh is well flavored, free from stringiness, and dry, like the Hubbard squash of years ago. Today's Hubbard squash are likely to be wet and stringy.

Summer squashes of all types are best cooked in a pressure saucepan. This cuts down the moisture required during cooking.

Winter squash may be cut into halves (nutmeg or acorn), or into pieces (Hubbard), and baked, or steamed.

Small pared pieces of Hubbard squash may be boiled, drained, and then mashed. Butternut squash may be cut into pieces, pared, and cooked in a pressure saucepan. The cooked squash is then mashed, seasoned, and made richer with added butter. Baking of butternut squash gives good results.

In preparing summer squash, the seeds are not removed, unless the squash is old.

In preparing winter squash, the seeds and surrounding loose membrane-like pith are scraped out and discarded.

SUMMER SQUASH WITH CREAM

Cook young, unpared pieces of summer squash in a pressure saucepan. Mash. Add a mixture of flour and cream shaken in a gravy mixer until smooth. Cook until the mixture thickens and loses raw-flour taste. Add plenty of butter and freshly ground pepper.

BAKED ACORN SQUASH

3 acorn squash	½ teaspoon salt
6 tablespoons honey or sirup	¾ teaspoon sausage meat

Wash and cut squash in halves. Remove fiber and seeds.

Place honey or sirup (maple preferred) and salt in halves of squash. Set the halves on a pan. Bake in a 375-degree oven for 15 minutes.

Add sausage meat. Continue baking for 30 minutes.
Serves 6.

SOUR CREAM SUMMER SQUASH

1 onion, sliced	2 pounds yellow squash
3 tablespoons margarine	1 cup thick sour cream

Sauté onion in hot fat. Cook about 5 minutes, or until soft.

Add sliced squash and continue cooking until lightly browned. Add sour cream and simmer until squash is tender. Season to taste. Sprinkle with paprika.
Serves 6.

BAKED SQUASH PARMESAN

1 acorn squash	Nutmeg
Salt and pepper	Margarine or butter
	Grated cheese

Wash and cut squash in half lengthwise. Remove seeds and fibers. Sprinkle the cut surface with salt, pepper, and nutmeg.

Place cut side down on a baking sheet. Bake at 400 degrees for 30 minutes.

Turn cut side up, brush with melted butter, and sprinkle generously with grated cheese. Continue baking for 15 minutes, or until squash is tender.

The squash can be baked as above and filled with creamed chicken and topped with a sprinkling of grated cheese.

Serves 6.

* * *

See also How To Freeze Vegetables and Home Canning of Vegetables.

Sweet Potatoes

Tʜɪs vegetable is a cousin of the morning glory and is totally unrelated to the Irish potato, despite the name.

A hot, moist climate is required for the best development of the sweet potato.

The pulp may be stringy and deep yellow or orange in color, with a reddish skin. This variety is called "yam" (botanically it is not a true yam).

When the skin is light buff in color and rather papery-looking, the sweet potato is of the Jersey variety. This kind has light yellow and dry or mealy pulp.

Sweet potatoes are poor keepers. Present custom calls for kiln-drying and/or waxing.

Bᴜʏɪɴɢ Gᴜɪᴅᴇ: Bright appearance; thick, chunky, medium size, tapered toward the ends. Common defects are greenish circular spots, damp appearance, sunken surface, and growth cracks.

Basic Rule for Cooking Sweet Potatoes

The sweet potato called "yam" is the one found in most markets today. Some years ago the popular potato was a "Jersey sweet."

Its skin was yellow to ocher in color. The pulp was mealy, dry, nutty in flavor. The color was a soft yellow.

The yam has a reddish skin. Its flesh is moist, stringy, wet, and a deep orange in color.

Both are cooked by baking or by boiling.

Wash or scrub potatoes lightly. Cook without cutting or paring in boiling salted water. Remove skin and traces of dark flesh. Serve "as is," or sliced and pan-fried.

When sweet potatoes are baked they are put whole and unpared in a 350-degree oven. If you test for doneness by squeezing, be sure to protect your hand and arm. Sweet potatoes frequently burst their skins. Prick the potato when baked to permit escape of steam. Serve skin and all. Have butter and salt at hand.

CANDIED SWEET POTATOES

Cook sweet potatoes in boiling salted water. Peel and cut in thick slices.

Put in layers in a baking dish. Dot generously with butter. Pour on maple sirup until it almost covers the slices.

Let stand overnight to absorb some of the sirup.

Next day, candy them by baking in a 300-degree oven until the slices are translucent. Turn the slices occasionally, so that they do not get too hard on top.

SWEET POTATOES WITH ORANGE

Boiled or baked sweet potatoes may be mashed, seasoned with orange juice and grated rind, enriched with butter, and beaten thoroughly until fluffy.

The mixture may be piled into the baked-potato shells or into scooped-out orange halves.

Brown the top lightly.

In place of orange juice, a few grains of nutmeg or cinnamon may be used.

SWEET POTATO BALLS

Leftover sweet potatoes may be mashed, shaped into balls, rolled in finely chopped peanuts, and browned in the oven.

CROQUETTES DE LUXE

2 cups mashed sweet potatoes   Salt and pepper
¼ cup blanched almonds   1 egg, beaten

Season sweet potatoes with salt and pepper and add beaten egg. Mix well. Add chopped almonds and mix. Chill thoroughly.

Form into croquettes and fry in deep fat.

Serves 4.

BANANA ALMOND SWEET POTATOES

4 cups mashed sweet potatoes   ½ cup brown sugar
1 cup almonds   ⅛ pound butter
1 cup mashed bananas   ¼ teaspoon salt
1 teaspoon cinnamon

Cook potatoes in boiling water. Pare and mash. Grate almonds, or chop fine. Add remaining ingredients. Blend to a smooth mixture.

Bake in a greased baking dish at 400 degrees for 20 to 30 minutes, or until the top is a light brown.

Serves 6.

SWEET POTATO PONE

4 cups grated raw sweet   ½ cup flour
  potatoes   ½ teaspoon nutmeg
1 egg   1 teaspoon cinnamon
¾ cup sorghum   ⅛ teaspoon cloves
4 tablespoons melted butter ¾ teaspoon salt
1 cup milk

Pare and grate sweet potatoes. Beat egg slightly. Add sorghum and butter to egg. Add to sweet potatoes.

Sift flour and measure. Add salt and spices. Sift again. Add dry ingredients and milk alternately to sweet potato mixture.

Bake in casserole at 275 degrees for 2½ hours, stirring occasionally during first 2 hours. Do not stir during the last half hour.

Serves 6.

SWEET POTATOES AND APPLES

6 sweet potatoes   ½ cup brown sugar
6 apples   ¼ cup butter
Maple sirup or water

Scrub and cook unpeeled sweet potatoes in boiling salted water. When done, peel.

Cut in slices ⅓ inch thick.

Place a layer of quartered peeled apples in bottom of baking dish. Sprinkle with brown sugar. Add one tablespoon butter. Cover with layer of sweet potatoes.

Repeat until baking dish is ⅔ full. Make top layer sweet potatoes. Add only enough water or maple sirup to cover the bottom of the dish.

Preheat oven to 350 degrees. Cover baking dish and set on lowest rack. At the end of 15 minutes, remove cover and continue baking until apples are shapeless, approximately 30 minutes longer.

Serves 6.

Swiss Chard

I<small>F</small> <small>YOU</small> are familiar with the growing beet plant you can visualize Swiss Chard. The plant does not develop an underground bulb, but puts all its energies into large leaves with a red or white midriff. Chard is cooked like other greens and like them is a good source of vitamins.

B<small>UYING</small> G<small>UIDE</small>: *See* Greens, page 99.

*　　*　　*

See How To Freeze Vegetables.

CHARD AND GREEN ONIONS

2 bunches Swiss chard
1 bunch green onions
½ teaspoon salt

¼ teaspoon monosodium
　glutamate
2 slices salt pork

Hard-cooked egg

Wash chard. Strip ribs from leaves and shred leaves. Cut cleaned onions (stems and all) into 2-inch lengths. Put in saucepan with salt pork. Add salt and monosodium glutamate. Cover tightly and cook slowly until chard is tender.

Remove salt-pork slices. Brown them. Put vegetables on hot serving dish. Top with browned salt pork and with sieved hard-cooked egg.

Serves 6.

RING OF SWISS CHARD WITH BABY CARROTS

4 cups Swiss chard	Carrots
1/3 cup butter	Salt
½ teaspoon salt	Pepper
Hard-cooked eggs	Hollandaise sauce (page 227)

Pick Swiss chard over carefully and wash thoroughly. Steam about 20 minutes. Drain and chop fine.

Measure cooked chard. Season with butter and salt. Press tightly into a buttered ring mold and keep warm until ready to serve.

Turn the mold onto a hot platter. Garnish the top with slices of hard-cooked eggs. Fill the center with baby carrots, buttered and seasoned with salt and pepper. Serve with Hollandaise sauce.

Serves 6.

Tomatoes are one of the showiest, best-tasting, most valuable, and most versatile of vegetables.

They may be yellow or red, small as cherries, or large enough to weigh a pound. Not too many years ago they were called "love apples" and considered poisonous. At that time they were grown for show, just as was the ornamental egg-plant. Now we use tomatoes as a beverage and in aspics and soups; they may be stewed, baked, escalloped, or served raw as a salad. Tomatoes may be made into marmalade, with ginger and lemon and sugar.

The number of acres on which tomatoes are grown is almost fantastic. This vegetable ranks high in favor, second only to the potato.

Buying Guide: Smooth, well rounded, plump, heavy for size, evenly colored, free from blemish, not overripe. Puffy or watery tomatoes are poor-flavored and wasteful; worm destruction is objectionable. Avoid fruit with ribby sections.

Basic Rule for Preparation of Tomatoes

Nature has been most kind to the tomato. Its gorgeous color is not lost in cooking. Its nutritive value is little changed. And the flavor of a cooked tomato is as acceptable as the flavor of a raw one. We might pat it on its back and say "Good dependable tomato."

Opinions differ. Shall it be skins on or off when served raw? Since skins are removed on occasions, three ways are suggested:

(1) Immerse tomato in boiling hot water for a minute or two. This loosens the skin so it may be removed easily.

(2) Impale tomato on fork. Twirl the tomato over an open flame until you hear the skin pop. The steam formed by this flash heat loosens the skin.

(3) Rub the surface of the tomato over and over with the blunt edge of a knife. This separates skin from pulp. Remove skin. This is the slowest method.

STEWED TOMATOES

Skin tomatoes and break them into pieces. Add salt and a few leaves of basil. Diced celery or onion may be added. Cook until the tomatoes are shapeless. Mellow the flavor, if necessary, with a suspicion of sugar.

COUNTRY STYLE TOMATOES

Stew tomatoes as directed in previous recipe. During cooking, add medium-sized cubes of bread. This dish is usually sweeter than plain stewed tomatoes.

ESCALLOPED TOMATOES

Put tomatoes in a casserole. Dot surface with butter. Season with basil, salt, pepper, and a bit of sugar. Top with freshly crumbed bread. Bake until the crumbs are nicely browned.

BROILED TOMATOES

Cut firm, ripe, medium-sized tomatoes crosswise. Sprinkle cut surface with salt and pepper. Dot with butter and sprinkle lightly with bread crumbs. Heat under the broiler 3 to 5 minutes, or until lightly browned. Take tomatoes from under broiler and sprinkle with grated cheese and return under heat until cheese is melted. Serve hot.

FRIED TOMATOES

6 ripe or green tomatoes	Salt and pepper
½ cup flour	6 slices bacon
	2 cups milk

Cut the tomatoes in half. Dip in flour well-seasoned with salt and pepper.

Fry the bacon crisp. Lift out. Fry the tomatoes in the bacon fat, turning once. When they are crusty brown, lift out onto platter.

Add remaining flour to fat in frying pan, stir well, and add milk to make gravy. The gravy should be quite thick.

Serves 6.

FRIED GREEN TOMATOES

Firm green tomatoes	Dry bread crumbs
2 cups cold water	Beaten egg
2 tablespoons salt	4 tablespoons butter

Select firm, sound green tomatoes and slice thin. Cover with water and salt and let stand one hour. Drain well and wipe dry on clean cloth.

Cover each slice of tomato with bread crumbs. Dip slice quickly into beaten egg and then into crumbs, to make an even coating on both sides.

Heat butter sizzling hot in skillet but avoid scorching it. Fry slices of tomatoes. Allow 6 minutes for frying first side, turn, and allow about 5 minutes for the other side. Maintain a heat which will fry tomatoes crisp quickly without scorching butter. Serve hot upon warm platter.

Serves 6.

TOMATO SURPRISE

8 tomatoes	1/16 teaspoon sugar
1 onion, minced	⅛ teaspoon pepper
½ pound mushrooms	¼ cup bread crumbs
3 tablespoons butter	2 eggs
½ teaspoon salt	Clove garlic

Wash tomatoes. Cut off tops and scoop out centers. Sauté minced onion and chopped mushrooms in butter. Add to tomato pulp and simmer 4 to 5 minutes.

Season and add bread crumbs. Add slightly beaten egg.

Heap mixture lightly into tomatoes. Top with tomato cover.

Place in baking dish and bake 30 minutes, or until brown. If garlic is used, rub frying pan with a clove before melting the butter.

Serves 8.

MODIFICATIONS OF BAKED STUFFED TOMATOES

TOMATOES WITH CELERY: Celery, onion, cheese, tapioca, salt, pepper.

TOMATOES WITH CRABMEAT: Crabmeat, bread crumbs, light cream, dry mustard, Worcestershire, sherry, salt, pepper, paprika.

TOMATOES WITH MACARONI OR RICE: Macaroni or rice, salt, pepper, paprika, thyme, chopped olives.

TOMATOES WITH MUSHROOMS AND CORN: Chopped onion, green pepper, mushrooms, kernel corn, egg, water, salt, pepper, celery salt.

TOMATOES WITH OKRA AND PEPPERS: Okra pods, chopped green pepper, dry bread crumbs, butter, onion, salt, pepper, paprika.

TOMATOES WITH OLIVES: Medium white sauce, sliced olives, hard-cooked eggs, crisp bacon, cayenne, curry powder, cheese sauce.

TOMATOES WITH OYSTERS: Celery salt, minced onion, oysters marinated in French dressing, buttered crumbs.

TOMATOES WITH SPINACH: Cooked spinach, melted butter, salt, onion, egg or oyster sauce.

TOMATOES WITH CORN: Crumbed bread, chopped onion and parsley, cheese.

TOMATOES WITH COTTAGE CHEESE: Cottage cheese, chopped nuts.

TOMATO TOAST

2 cups tomatoes	3 tablespoons flour
½ cup water	½ teaspoon salt
1 tablespoon minced parsley	Cayenne
3 allspice berries	½ teaspoon dry mustard
3 peppercorns	¼ pound grated cheese
3 tablespoons bacon fat	1 egg
1 small onion, sliced	Hot buttered toast

Simmer tomatoes, water, minced parsley, crushed allspice berries, and peppercorns in a covered saucepan about 15 minutes.

Brown the sliced onion in bacon fat. Add flour, salt and cayenne, dry mustard. Add this to the tomato mixture. Stir well over fire until boiling point is reached. Strain.

Add the grated cheese. Stir over fire until blended. Add the beaten egg. Stir very rapidly until egg slightly thickens the mixture. Pour over hot buttered toast. Serve immediately.

Serves 6.

TOMATO DUMPLINGS

4 cups spicy tomato juice
1 cup biscuit mix
½ cup milk

Combine biscuit mix and milk. Stir until blended.

Bring tomato juice to boil. Drop dough from a teaspoon into hot juice. Cover saucepan and cook for 12 minutes.

Serves 4.

TOMATO BUTTERMILK COOLER

Combine ⅓ to ½ cup chilled tomato juice with ½ to ⅔ cup cold buttermilk. Salt to taste.

TOMATO JUICE COCKTAIL

2 cups tomato juice
½ teaspoon onion
1 teaspoon celery
¼ teaspoon Worcestershire
   sauce
2 tablespoons lemon juice
½ teaspoon sugar
½ teaspoon salt
½ teaspoon horse-radish

This is especially good when juice from fresh tomatoes is used.

Combine tomato juice, grated onion, chopped celery, and all seasonings. Chill for 1 hour. Strain.

Serves 4 to 6.

TOMATO CHEESE PUFF

2¼ cups tomato juice
½ pound Cheddar cheese
6 slices toast

Cover bottom of baking dish with 3 slices of toast. Sprinkle with half of shredded cheese.

Cover with remaining toast and cheese. Pour hot tomato juice over top and bake 20 minutes at 375 degrees.

Serves 6.

GREEN TOMATO MINCE MEAT

3 pounds green tomatoes
1 tablespoon salt
3 pounds apples
1 pound brown sugar
2 puonds seedless raisins
1 cup ground suet

1 tablespoon nutmeg
1 tablespoon grated lemon rind
2½ tablespoons cinnamon
2 teaspoons ground cloves
¼ cup vinegar

Grind tomatoes. Add salt. Let stand 1 hour. Drain.

Cook tomatoes in water to cover for 5 minutes. Drain.

Add pared, cored, and chopped apples. Add remaining ingredients. Simmer for 1 hour.

Fill hot sterilized jars. Seal.

Serves 6.

ALPINE SANDWICH *

12 slices toast
Mayonnaise
6 slices Swiss cheese
Mustard
3 tomatoes

Salt
Paprika
6 slices broiled bacon
Leaf lettuce
French dressing (page 215)

* Recipe by Marye Dahnke, author of *The Cheese Cook Book.*

Spread mayonnaise on 6 slices of toast. Cover with a slice of cheese. Spread with mustard. Top with 2 slices of tomato, salt, paprika, a slice of broiled bacon, and a lettuce leaf dipped in French dressing.

Cover with a slice of toast. Cut diagonally.

*   *   *

Additional recipes for tomatoes will be found under Appetizers, Pickles and Relishes, Salads, Soups, and Home Canning of Vegetables.

London daily hears my cry—
Turnips, carrots, who will buy?
White turnips, turnips white,
Young carrots, ho.

Aɴᴅ ʟᴏɴᴅᴏɴᴇʀs in the seventeenth century did hear the turnip vendor crying his wares as he walked up and down the streets of London Town.

Francis Wheatley, R.A., is the English artist who romanticized the itinerant vendor in a series of paintings bearing the title "Cries of London." Milkmaids, scissors grinders, menders of chairs, purveyors of sweet China oranges filled the air from morning to night with the musical calling of their wares.

[176]

Turnips are known as one of the root-stock vegetables. They have a certain earthiness of flavor which makes them an excellent vegetable to serve at a holiday dinner where the rich turkey dressing and gravy need a flavor foil. The leaves of turnips are classed as greens. A dish called "hog jowl and turnip greens" is of Southern origin.

BUYING GUIDE: Few leaf scars around the crown; few fibrous roots around the base; heavy for size; smooth and firm. Tops should be fresh, clean, crisp, and tender. Wilted, coarse, and yellowed leaves usually stringy and tough. Examine for lice and decay. Leaves do not indicate quality of root, because they deteriorate quickly. Coarse overgrown turnips may be tough, woody, and strong in flavor.

Basic Rules for Cooking Turnips

Turnips are an excellent vegetable to serve with roast pork, roast fresh ham, roast poultry. They have a down-to-earth flavor that cuts richness. In addition, they have a pungency or "spark" that their heavier cousin, rutabaga, lacks.

Wash the turnips. Pare. Cut into pieces, leave whole, or cut into cubes. Turnips may be rather porous or spongy inside. This is noticeable when you cut them. Discard the spongy pieces.

Cook in rapidly boiling salted water or in pressure saucepan. Drain and serve hot.

BUTTERED TURNIPS

Cooked cubed turnips may be dressed with melted butter.

TURNIPS IN CREAM

Dress cooked cubed turnips with a small amount of cream.

MASHED TURNIPS

Mash cooked turnips. Add butter and a suspicion of sugar.

SAUTÉED TURNIP QUARTERS

Drain cooked turnip quarters. Sauté in bacon fat. Serve with crisp bacon slices.

*   *   *

Additional recipes for turnips will be found under Soups and How To Freeze Vegetables.

*   *   *

TURNIP GREENS (*see* Greens, page 99).

Watercress

WATERCRESS is popularly used as a garnish, but like parsley it should be eaten, not just pushed aside. Thin-leaved, deep-green watercress is vitamin-rich. Its peppery spiciness adds zest to dishes in which it is used. Watercress should be well washed in cold water to remove sand and slugs. Discard slender rootlets. Break the plant into small sprigs.

BUYING GUIDE: *See* Greens.

* * *

See Appetizers and Salads.

Zucchini

THIS long, slender, green-skinned summer squash is growing in popularity and use. See page 158 for a general discussion of squash and buying guide.

Zucchini need not be pared unless they are overmature.

Scrub them well. The skin, especially toward the stem end, is slightly rough. It holds sand and grit which are not seen by the eye, but which are noticeable after the zucchini has been cooked.

Cut zucchini into inch-thick slices. Parboil these in rapidly boiling salted water, or cook them in a pressure saucepan. Like all summer squashes, zucchini cooks quickly. Avoid overcooking.

SAUTÉED ZUCCHINI SLICES

Drain the parboiled slices. Sauté in bacon fat on hot griddle. Brown both sides. Serve hot.

SAUTÉED RAW ZUCCHINI SLICES

Wash and slice zucchini in slices about ¼ inch thick. Sauté these in small amount of hot fat. Have the heat rather low, since cooking and browning are carried on simultaneously.

ZUCCHINI HAM CASSEROLE

½ cup raw rice	2 tablespoons cooking oil
4 zucchini	Salt and pepper
1 chopped onion	¾ cup grated Romano cheese
1 cup ground cooked ham	2 tablespoons butter
2 eggs	1 cup soft bread crumbs

Wash the rice and cook in one quart of boiling, salted water. Drain. Cook the zucchini in a small amount of boiling salted water until tender. Do not overcook. Drain and chop coarsely.

Combine the rice and zucchini with the onion, ham, beaten eggs, oil, salt and pepper to taste, and ½ cup of cheese.

Pour into a casserole and sprinkle with the remaining cheese and the crumbs, which have been tossed in the butter. Bake at 325 degrees for 40 minutes.

Serves 6.

BAKED ZUCCHINI

1½ pounds zucchini	1 teaspoon salt
3 tablespoons butter	1/16 teaspoon pepper
¼ teaspoon minced garlic	1 cup tomatoes
2/3 cup minced onion	½ cup shredded cheese
½ cup diced green pepper	2 tablespoons bread crumbs

Cut the zucchini into ¼-inch slices without peeling. Steam them until tender.

Melt butter in a skillet and add the garlic, onion, green pepper, seasonings, and tomato. Cook until tender. Combine with the squash and cheese.

Pour the mixture into a greased casserole and sprinkle with bread crumbs. Bake at 350 degrees for 15 minutes.

Serves 6.

ZUCCHINI PROVENÇALE

6 zucchini
1 onion
4 tablespoons cooking oil
2 cups cut-up tomatoes

1 green pepper, cut fine
1 clove garlic
Salt and pepper
Grated Parmesan cheese

Wash zucchini and cut, unpared, into thick slices, or large cubes. Set aside.

Sauté sliced onion in oil in heavy frying pan. Add tomatoes and green pepper and juice expressed from one clove of garlic. Simmer for 10 minutes.

Add cubed zucchini. Cover the pan and cook until zucchini is tender. Season to taste.

Just before serving, sprinkle with grated cheese. Chopped parsley may be added if desired.

VARIATION: Curled anchovies may be put on top of mixture a few moments before removing from fire.

Serves 6.

Appetizers

ALL TOO frequently appetizers belie their name and are not appetite teasers, but appetite spoilers.

If a cocktail round or two precedes a dinner, the food offered with the drinks should be light and flavor-provocative but not filling.

A different situation exists when the guests are counting on getting enough food from a buffet array for a meal.

Alcoholic beverages as well as vegetable juices seem to call for highly flavored, salty, crunchy appetizers. Fruity beverages are happier with canapés, or accompaniments that are fairly sweet and somewhat bland in flavor.

The number of appetizers in this book is small. The ones suggested are at home on the relish tray placed on the dinner table as well as on the cocktail buffet table.

Crunchiness, flavor with a capital F, "pretty to look at"

are the qualities used as a basis for selection of the appetizers given here.

BEET RELISH

4 cups cooked beets	¼ cup sugar
½ cup chopped onion	¾ cup vinegar
2 tablespoons freshly grated horse-radish	Salt and pepper

Chop cooked beets fine. Add chopped onion.
Bring remaining ingredients to boil. Pour over beets. Cool.

CUCUMBER CHEESE SPREAD

6 ounces cream cheese	½ teaspoon salt
2 tablespoons mayonnaise	¼ teaspoon celery salt
3 tablespoons shredded cucumber	1/16 teaspoon paprika

Blend all ingredients together and use as an appetizer spread, or a sandwich filling.
Makes 1 cup.

STUFFED CUCUMBER APPETIZER

Cucumber	½ teaspoon Worcestershire sauce
3 ounces cream cheese	
2 teaspoons mayonnaise	1 tablespoon cut chives
Salt and pepper	

Select plump, straight cucumber. Core the cucumber the entire length. Score outside by running prongs of fork lengthwise over surface.

Mix cheese, mayonnaise, sauce, chives, and seasonings. Stuff cored cucumber. Chill.

At serving time, cut into ¼ inch thick slices. Place on crackers. Serve with cream of tomato soup, or with cocktails.

CELERY WHIRLS

Celery
Pimiento cream cheese spread

Lettuce
French dressing

Cut the tops from a bunch of celery, wash, and dry the separated stalks. Stuff the smallest stalk with the cheese spread. Fill the next larger stalk and press it onto the first. Continue thus with all the stalks, pressing each one onto the last. Tie completed bunch with string; chill. To serve, cut in slices with a sharp knife.

Serve on lettuce with French dressing as a salad; or alone as a relish or an appetizer.

GENTLEMEN'S SPREAD

1 small onion
1 tablespoon green pepper
3 tablespoons deviled ham
3 tablespoons liver sausage
1 tablespoon dill pickle

1 teaspoon Worcestershire sauce
Dash of paprika
6 ounces processed soft yellow cheese or cream cheese

Chop onion, green pepper, deviled ham, liver sausage, dill pickle, and mix with Worcestershire sauce and paprika.

Mash cheese and cream it as you would cream shortening. Mix with other ingredients and shape into balls. The yellow cheese is more readily creamed if it has been allowed to soften slightly in a warm kitchen.

These balls are easily spread upon crisp, salty crackers.

ROQUEFORT STUFFED CELERY

4½ ounces Roquefort cheese
3 ounces cream cheese
1 teaspoon Worcestershire sauce

½ teaspoon salt
1/16 teaspoon cayenne
10 stalks celery

1 tablespoon mayonnaise

Blend the Roquefort and cream cheese together. Add the seasonings.

Fill the grooves of small crisp celery stalks with this mixture.

Serves 6.

CAULIFLOWER CHEESE SPREAD

½ cup chopped cauliflower, raw
1½ tablespoons sweet pickle, chopped
1/3 cup celery, chopped
3 ounces cream cheese

¼ teaspoon salt
¼ teaspoon Worcestershire sauce
¼ teaspoon celery salt
1/16 teaspoon pepper
1 teaspoon grated onion

Rye bread

Chop cauliflower, sweet pickle, and celery very fine. Combine with all other ingredients.

Spread on slices of rye bread.

Serves 6.

WATERCRESS CREAM CHEESE SPREAD

3 ounces cream cheese
¼ cup chopped watercress

Blend the cream cheese until soft and fluffy. Add the watercress and mix thoroughly. Season to taste, using salt, monosodium glutamate. Worcestershire sauce.

GREEN GODDESS DIP FOR CHIPS

1 clove garlic, grated
2 tablespoons anchovy paste
3 tablespoons finely chopped chives
1 tablespoon lemon juice
1 tablespoon tarragon wine vinegar

½ cup heavy sour cream
1 cup mayonnaise
1/3 cup finely chopped parsley
Coarse salt
Coarsely ground black pepper

Combine ingredients in order given. Pour in serving bowl and chill.

Canned whole anchovies may be chopped fine and substituted for the anchovy paste. Coarse salt may be purchased in pound containers. Lacking a pepper grinder, use a pestle to mash the peppercorns in a mortar.

GUACAMOLE *

2 fresh tomatoes, small	¼ cup mayonnaise
2 ripe avocados	1 three-ounce package cream
1 small onion, grated	cheese
1 tablespoon red wine vinegar	Salt
Freshly ground black pepper	

Peel and mash the tomatoes and avocados together. Add the other ingredients and blend well.

Do not prepare too far in advance as the mixture darkens on standing.

* Pronounced wah-ka-mo-leh.

Pickles and Relishes

GRANDMA's fruit cellar might well have been called "winter treasure." Here were canned fruits; brandied tutti frutti; jars of apple butter; kegs of sauerkraut; crocks of pickles; mysterious jampots and bottles of catsup, sealing wax topped; colorful and flavorful piccalilli and softer-colored corn salad.

Meals of potatoes, fried salt pork, turnips, and carrots lose some of the monotony when accented with homemade relishes and pickles.

Commercial concerns with scientific "know how" produce pickles, big and small, sweet, sour, and dill flavor of uniform quality. Quantity production never seems to give these pickles a factory flavor. But no commercial concern will ever be able to make superior relishes with homemade texture and taste and do it at a price most of us can afford.

The recipes in this section are but a sampling of what

may be done better in the home kitchen than in the factory.

Chili sauce and catsup recipes are given. Tomato marmalade that has the zest of lemon and of ginger. Carrots and pumpkin may be transformed similarly. If you are of an experimental mind, try adapting the tomato recipe for other vegetable marmalades.

The Jerusalem artichoke pickle is a novelty to most Northerners. It is quite popular south of the Mason and Dixon Line.

BORDEAUX SAUCE

4 quarts green tomatoes	1 ounce whole allspice
6 quarts cabbage	1 tablespoon whole cloves
12 green peppers	1 ounce ground ginger
12 medium onions	1 ounce celery seed
¾ pound brown sugar	4 quarts cider vinegar
½ cup whole mustard seed	Salt

Chop tomatoes, cabbage, peppers (freed from seeds and pith), onions.

Add remaining ingredients. Cook for ½ hour. Salt to taste. Pour while hot in jars. Seal.

PICKLED PEPPERS

9 large yellow pickling peppers	1½ tablespoons salt
1½ cups white vinegar	1 to 2 tablespoons mixed spices
1½ cups water	Garlic, if desired

Mix vinegar, water, salt, and spices. Boil for 5 minutes. Wash and drain the peppers. Remove the stem end and pith with seeds, Cut in lengthwise sections, or leave whole. If desired, put 1 washed whole *hot* pepper in the clean hot jar with the seeded peppers.

Pour the boiled liquid over the peppers to fill the jars to overflowing. Add a piece of garlic if desired. Cap tightly. Set away for at least 2 weeks to ripen.

The peppers are crisp and well flavored after 2 weeks in the jar. There is no fermentation.

The amount of liquid is sufficient for one quart jar and one pint jar of peppers.

CRYSTAL PICKLES

Wash 25 six-inch freshly picked cucumbers (should be less than 24 hours from the vine), leaving ¼- to ½-inch stems. Place in a stone crock and cover with this brine:

Pickle Brine

> 4 cups pickling salt (not iodized table salt)
> 1 gallon water (16 cups)

Cover with a plate and weight plate down by filling a large fruit jar with water and setting this on the plate. Cover the stone crock with thin muslin. Skim daily if necessary. Leave for 2 weeks. Drain cucumbers and wash well in cold water.

Cut into thick slices and cover with cold water to which 2 tablespoons powdered alum has been added, stirring the water until the alum is well dissolved. Let stand in this alum water for at least 24 hours (a little longer if too salty). Drain and wash again and put into a stone crock.

Make a sirup, using ingredients below. Bring sirup to a boil. Pour while hot over the cucumber slices.

Sirup

1 quart cider vinegar	2 quarts sugar
2 long sticks cinnamon, broken into pieces (in spice bag)	1 teaspoon whole cloves
	1 teaspoon powdered mace

Repeat for 4 more mornings—drain the sirup from the cucumbers, heat sirup to the boiling point and pour over the chunky slices, leaving the spice bag in until the pickles are finished. On the last morning, cut each chunk into 3 slices. Can cold in sterilized jars. The jars do not need to be sealed.

SUSAN'S DILL PICKLES

36 cucumbers (slender 5-inch ones)
Dill
1 cup white vinegar
2 cups water
1 to 2 tablespoons mixed spices
1½ teaspoons salt
Garlic (optional)

Wash cucumbers and soak in brine, using ½ cup salt to each gallon of water. After 6 to 12 hours' soaking, drain off the brine and rinse the pickles in cold water. Drain or wipe the pickles dry.

Pack them in clean jars, getting them in as tightly as possible. Stuff a large spray of washed dill blossoms into each jar.

Make spicy vinegar mixture. For 2 cups water and 1 cup vinegar use 1½ tablespoons salt and 2 tablespoons mixed spices.

Boil this mixture for 5 minutes. Pour, boiling hot, over the cucumbers packed in the jar. Fill to overflowing. Add a clove of peeled garlic if desired. Adjust the rubber ring and screw down the zinc cap. Process in boiling water for 10 minutes. Each quart jar takes about 1 cup of the above liquid.

SUN DILL PICKLES

Use cucumbers within 24 hours after picking. Wash and drain. Soak overnight in enough brine to cover them. Make the brine by using ½ cup of salt in each gallon of cold water.

Next morning, drain and rinse the cucumbers and pack

into clean, hot jars. Discard brine. Crush two or more stalks of dill down into each jar. Add a clove of garlic if desired.

Make a fresh brine by using ½ cup salt for each gallon of water. Boil for 3 minutes. When cool, pour into the jars. Seal them and set them in the sun. Turn jars and transfer to a shady spot occasionally. Liquid will ooze out of the jars and the liquid inside will become quite murky. After two days in the sun, remove to the house. Fermentation will continue for about a week and the murky liquid will clear. When opened, the pickles will have the flattish dill flavor associated with the best commercially made dills.

ARTICHOKE PICKLE

2 quarts Jerusalem artichokes	1¼ cups sugar
Cold brine to cover	2 teaspoons turmeric
1 small clove garlic	2 tablespoons pickling spice
1 quart vinegar	

Scrub artichokes. If roots are large, cut into fair-sized pieces. Soak overnight in brine made by using the proportion of 1 cup salt to 1 gallon of water. Rinse, drain, and pack into clean jars.

Combine garlic, sugar, turmeric, pickling spice, and vinegar. Let mixture simmer for 15 minutes. Then let the mixture boil for about 10 minutes.

Pour over the artichokes in the jars. Fill jars to overflowing with liquid. Seal.

SWEET PICKLED ONIONS

10 pounds pickling onions
Salt

Pickling sirup

1 quart white vinegar	1½ cups sugar
2 cups water	1 ounce mixed pickling spices

Peel onions and place in a crock container.

Using the proportion of ½ cup salt to 1 quart of water, make enough brine to cover the onions. Heat to the boiling point and while still boiling hot, pour over the onions, completely covering them. Keep onions under the brine by weighting them down with a plate. Let stand 24 hours.

Next day drain and rinse in cold water. Pack tightly in clean jars.

Combine vinegar and water with sugar and spices which have been tied in a bag. Bring to a boil slowly and pour hot over the onions, filling the jar to the top with sirup. Seal tightly.

NOTE: A few pieces of julienne red pepper may be put in each jar for color.

BREAD AND BUTTER PICKLES

12 cucumbers, 6 to 7 inches long	½ teaspoon turmeric
8 small white onions	½ teaspoon ground cloves
2 green peppers	2 teaspoons mustard seed
½ cup salt	1 teaspoon celery seed
Ice	5 cups vinegar, medium strength
5 cups sugar	

Wash the cucumbers. Slice them thin—paper thin. You will have approximately 1 gallon, or 16 cups. Slice the onions and shred the green peppers from which you have taken the seeds and pith. Pack these with the salt and some cracked ice. Weight the vegetables down. Let stand 3 hours.

Drain, rinse quickly, and drain thoroughly. If you don't there will be excess liquid. Make a pickling sirup using the sugar, turmeric, cloves, seeds, and vinegar. Boil for 5 minutes. Add the drained vegetables. Bring the whole mixture to the simmering point, not the boiling point. Pack in clean hot jars and cap at once.

PICCALILLI

1 gallon green tomatoes
1 head cabbage
3 sweet green peppers
2 large onions
½ cup salt

1 cup brown sugar
2 tablespoons mustard seed
1 tablespoon celery seed
1 tablespoon horse-radish
1 quart vinegar

Chop and mix vegetables with the salt. Let stand overnight. Drain. Mix sugar, seasonings, and vinegar. Boil 1 minute. Add vegetables. Heat to boiling. Pack into hot jars and seal at once.

CORN RELISH OR SALAD

1½ dozen ears corn
1 small cabbage, chopped
1 bunch celery
4 onions, sliced thin
2 green peppers, chopped
2 quarts vinegar

2 cups sugar
1 cup flour
½ cup salt
½ teaspoon mustard
¼ teaspoon cayenne
½ teaspoon turmeric

Cut corn from cob. Separate celery stalks, remove leaves, and chop. Put vegetables in kettle and pour over half the vinegar. Mix sugar, flour, salt, mustard, cayenne, and turmeric and add remaining vinegar. Combine mixtures, bring to the boiling point, and simmer 40 minutes.

PHILADELPHIA RELISH

2 cups finely chopped cabbage
1 cup finely chopped celery
½ green pepper, chopped fine
1 tablespoon sugar

2 teaspoons salt
½ teaspoon celery seed
¼ cup vinegar
Lemon cups

Chop the cabbage, celery, and green pepper "exceedingly fine." Add sugar, salt, celery seed, and vinegar.

Let stand in cool place for 24 hours.

Cut lemons in halves, crosswise. Remove pulp. Use shells only. Put relish in shells for individual service.

It may be necessary to cut a thin slice from the bottom of the lemon shell to give it a firm base.

NOTE: This relish should be served within a day of making. It cannot be preserved in jars or cans.

Salads

Sidney smith referred to salad as "an herbaceous treat." Moderns are likely to toss both the word and the salad around more casually.

Salad is an accepted "must" for today's dinners and buffet meals. A jellied salad—the love and pet of ladies' club luncheons—is quite likely to be the peeve of men who want something less sweet, less dessertlike. After all, a salad is an interlude between a rich main course and the sweet or dessert.

Vegetable salads may be substantial mixtures like potato salad, simple affairs like cole slaw, perky greens in a tossed mixture, or unimaginative head lettuce, sectioned and almost covered with Thousand Island dressing. (Most men are devoted to this unimaginative lettuce combination.)

The common denominator of all salads should be flavor:

zesty, appetite-teasing. The dressing should dominate most salads.

Leafy greens lose perkiness soon after the salad dressings are added. This is because of the acidity and saltiness of dressings, or of added ingredients such as bits of herring or anchovy. This precludes mixing salads far ahead of serving time.

"Dressing a salad" or "fatiguing the greens" are phrases used to describe the process of coating leafy greens with oil and vinegar (or some variation of a French dressing). This should be done lightly, lest the leaves be mashed and broken. A wooden salad bowl, and wooden or horn salad spoon and fork are less destructive of leafy structure than china bowls and silver mixing spoons.

If a salad is "dressed" at the table, be sure the bowl in which the mixing will be done is large. Otherwise the greens spill over. Also, individual salad bowls need to be of generous size and for the same reason.

Since plenty of zest and tang is essential to a good salad the leafy greens must be well drained before they are put into the salad bowl, otherwise the flavor is diluted.

No salad should be pallid or colorless. Tomatoes, radishes, paprika, fresh or canned pimiento, fresh herb leaves, chopped chives, parsley, water cress, green peppers, lettuce itself, stuffed green olives, capers, glistening black olives, sieved hard-cooked egg yolk, egg white, yellow Cheddar cheese, grated raw carrot, toasted nutmeats—any of these may be used to add color and eye appeal.

Salad accompaniments may be cheese straws; Melba toast; garlic bread; potato chips; cheese puffs; crisp crackers—plain or herb-buttered and toasted or buttered and spread with sesame seeds and then lightly toasted. These various accompaniments have one thing in common—they are crunchy or crackly.

Salads should be pictures, but pictorial ones are never served at smart tables. Pictorial ones—those food combinations made to look like candles in candle sticks, "raggedy Anns or Andys," butterflies, Halloween masks, are a mistake. After all, we are not accustomed to eating candlewax, butterflies, or humans, so why expect us to eat reasonable facsimiles thereof?

Keep salads simple; never make them look manhandled, beribboned, or beflounced.

MOTHER'S POTATO SALAD

8 medium potatoes
1 cup cooked salad dressing (page 217)
½ cup mayonnaise
¼ cup heavy cream, whipped
½ cucumber, diced

2 cups diced celery
2 tablespoons grated onion
¼ cup chopped green onions (optional)
2 hard-cooked eggs, sliced

SUGGESTED GARNISHES: radishes, parsley, green pepper, 2 hard-cooked eggs (in addition to the two used in the salad).

NOTE: Before mixing the salad, read the method.

Cook the potatoes in boiling water. Peel and cut in ¼-inch slices.

Combine cooked salad dressing (page 217), mayonnaise, and cream.

Add half of the above dressing to the hot potatoes. Add remaining half of dressing to cucumber, celery, onion.

Combine the potatoes, vegetables, and sliced egg lightly. Set in refrigerator until serving time.

Place in lettuce-lined salad bowl. Garnish as desired.

To prevent mashing the eggs, they are added after the potatoes and the other vegetables have been combined with the dressing. Mixing is done lightly.

Radish roses, Julienne green pepper, parsley, sieved hard-cooked egg yolks, and sieved hard-cooked egg whites are always decorative.

Serves 6.

GLOBE ARTICHOKE SALAD

Cooked artichokes	Mayonnaise *or*
Crabmeat	Thousand Island dressing
Celery	(page 218)

Wash artichokes. Cut off and discard about ½ inch of tops of leaves. Tie a string around each artichoke to keep leaves together while being cooked. Cook in boiling salted water until bottom of artichoke can be pierced easily with fork tines.

Remove from water, invert, and drain.

When cool, scoop out part of pulpy center. Remove spiny choke.

Mix cubed pulp with cooked crabmeat and diced celery. Combine with mayonnaise or Thousand Island dressing. Serve cold.

ASPARAGUS SALAD

Asparagus stalks	Rings of green pepper
French dressing (page 215)	Lettuce

Cook and drain stalks of asparagus. Marinate in French dressing for ½ hour.

Place 3 to 5 stalks in a green-pepper ring. Place on lettuce. Dress with additional French dressing.

STRING BEAN SALAD

Marinate cooked string beans in French dressing (*See* page 215) ½ hour. Drain and arrange 8 or 9 beans in a lengthwise bundle.

Place on lettuce. Band the bundle with a narrow strip of red pimiento. Serve with additional French dressing.

HEAD LETTUCE WITH ROQUEFORT DRESSING

5 ounces Roquefort-cheese spread
4 wedges head lettuce
Salad dressing

Soften the cheese spread by letting it come to room temperature, then mash and beat until creamy. Measure an equal amount of salad dressing and slowly blend it with the cheese spread. Mix thoroughly and chill.

Place lettuce wedges on crisp lettuce on individual plates and serve with the Roquefort dressing.

Serves 6.

WESTERN SALAD BOWL

¼ cup salad oil
2 cloves garlic
2 cups bread cubes
2 quarts salad greens
1 tablespoon Worcestershire sauce
6 tablespoons salad oil

¼ teaspoon black pepper
½ teaspoon salt
¼ cup grated Parmesan cheese
¼ cup crumbled Blue cheese
3½ tablespoons lemon juice
1 egg. Cook in boiling water for 1 minute.

Combine ¼ cup of salad oil with garlic and let stand at room temperature several hours.

Toast bread cubes until golden brown. Do this in shallow pan in 250-degree oven. Turn cubes often with fork.

Wash greens, dry well, tear into edible-sized pieces. Put in a salad bowl. Chill them until serving time.

Combine the next seven ingredients. Add to the greens, tossing them lightly.

Break over the greens. Remove garlic from salad oil. Discard garlic. Mix oil and toasted bread cubes. Add to salad, toss again lightly.

If desired, add 8 anchovies just before the last tossing.

This is a variation of Caesar Salad.

Serves 6.

TOMATO AND AVOCADO SALAD BOWL

3 tomatoes
1 avocado
½ cup French dressing
  (page 215)

1 head lettuce
2 ounces Blue cheese

Peel the tomatoes and cut into eighths. Cut the avocado in half and remove the seed. Peel and slice. Marinate the tomato and avocado in the dressing for ½ hour in refrigerator. Drain.

Break the lettuce into small pieces.

Crumble the cheese. Arrange in alternate layers in a salad bowl. Pour the dressing from the marinated tomatoes and avocado over all and toss lightly. Serve from the bowl.

Serves 6.

RED, WHITE, AND GREEN SALAD

1 pound cabbage
1 cucumber
1 green pepper

French dressing (page 215)
Tomatoes
Mayonnaise

Shred cabbage. Cut cucumber and green pepper into matchlike pieces. Mix and marinate in dressing.

Serve garnished with quartered tomatoes. Pass mayonnaise with salad.

Serves 6.

BEET SALAD DELICIOUS

4 cups cubed cooked beets
½ cup French dressing
  (page 215)
3 sweet pickles *or*
4 tablespoons relish

2 green onions and tops
1 cup diced celery
Escarole
2 eggs, hard-cooked

Marinate cubed cooked beets in French dressing. At serving time, drain.

Add chopped pickles or pickle relish, minced onions, and celery. Serve on escarole and garnish with egg slices.

Serves 6.

STUFFED TOMATO SALAD

2 green peppers
1 onion
1 cucumber
2 cups cottage cheese

Salt and pepper
5 tomatoes
Lettuce
French dressing (page 215)

Chop the green peppers, onion, and cucumber. Blend these with the cheese. Add the salt and pepper.

For each serving, peel a firm tomato and cut it poinsettia-style into 5 sections, almost to the stem end.

Place each tomato on crisp lettuce. Press the sections slightly apart. Fill center with the cottage cheese mixture. Serve with French dressing.

Serves 6.

TOMATO ROSE SALAD *

2 tomatoes
3 ounces cream cheese
Milk

1 egg yolk
Watercress
French dressing (page 215)

* Recipe by Marye Dahnke, author of *The Cheese Cook Book.*

Peel tomatoes and chill.

Slightly soften cream cheese with milk.

Form 2 rows of petals on each tomato by pressing level teaspoons of the cheese against the side of the tomato, then drawing the teaspoon down with a curving motion.

Sprinkle the center of each tomato with hard-cooked egg yolk pressed through a strainer. Serve on watercress with dressing.

Serves 6.

TOMATO ANCHOVY SALAD

Lettuce or watercress	6 rolled anchovies
2 tomatoes	1 teaspoon lemon juice
1 Bermuda onion	1 egg yolk, hard-cooked

French dressing (page 215)

Arrange lettuce on 6 salad plates. Peel tomatoes and cut into 3 slices. Place 1 slice on each plate; cover with a thin slice of onion. Top with an anchovy.

Sprinkle with lemon juice and garnish with sieved hard-cooked egg yolk. Serve with French dressing.

Serves 6.

STUFFED TOMATOES IN FROZEN DRESSING

6 tomatoes	2 tablespoons chives
1 teaspoon salt	1 cup cottage cheese
¾ cup cucumber	1 cup salad dressing
3 tablespoons green pepper	1 cup heavy cream

Lettuce

Wash tomatoes, remove skins. Hollow out centers. Sprinkle with salt and invert and chill.

Mix grated cucumber, minced green pepper, and chives with cheese and 3 tablespoons of dressing.

Pack mixture into tomatoes. Arrange tomatoes upside down in a row in freezing tray.

Fold whipped cream into remaining dressing, pour over tomatoes, and freeze about 2 hours.

Cut frozen mixture into squares around each tomato and serve each square on a lettuce leaf.

Serves 6.

ROMAINE SALAD

2 heads romaine
12 small beets, cooked
Prepared horse-radish

Roquefort salad dressing
(page 215)

Wash and drain romaine. Tear into salad-size pieces.

Make small cavity in top of each beet by scooping out a small amount, using the tip of a teaspoon. Fill cavities with horse-radish.

Place romaine on individual salad plates. Place beets on romaine. Dress with Roquefort salad dressing.

Serves 6.

SLICED TOMATOES, 1890 STYLE

4 tomatoes
½ cup vinegar

1 tablespoon sugar
1 tablespoon onion (optional)
Salt and pepper

Peel and slice ripe tomatoes. Dress with vinegar, sugar, salt, and pepper.

NOTE: If vinegar seems strong use less and dilute it with water. Chopped or sliced onion may be added if desired.

Serves 6.

KIDNEY BEAN SALAD

1 cup cooked kidney beans	1 cup Cheddar cheese
3 tablespoons chopped onion	Salt and pepper
½ cup celery	Lettuce
1 cup diced apple	Mayonnaise

Drain cooked beans. Chop onion. Dice celery and apple. (If desired, the skin of the apple may be left on. This adds a note of color if red apples have been chosen.) Cube the cheese.

Combine ingredients, season, and mix lightly.

Serve on lettuce with mayonnaise.

NOTE: Raw apples discolor quickly when cut. You may want to marinate the small cubes of apple in French dressing (*See* page 215) before putting them with the remainder of the salad.

Serves 6.

CHEF'S SALAD

3 cups salad greens	½ cup French dressing
1 cup boiled ham	(page 215)
1 cup cooked chicken	Mayonnaise (optional)
1 cup Swiss cheese	Salt and pepper
½ cup Roquefort or Blue cheese	12 anchovies

Wash and drain salad greens and tear them into small pieces. (Lettuce, romaine, curly endive are suggested.)

Cut cooked ham, cooked chicken, and Swiss cheese, into matchlike strips. Crumble Roquefort cheese.

Put above ingredients in a salad bowl. Dress with French dressing, adding mayonnaise if desired. Toss lightly, lest you crush the greens. Season. Anchovies are salty and wilt the greens quickly. Do not add them, or the dressing, until serving time.

Serves 6.

PIQUANT SALAD BOWL

1 head lettuce
1 head curly endive
1 bunch watercress

1 clove garlic, optional
½ pound Swiss cheese
¼ cup chili sauce

½ cup Piquant French dressing (page 215)

Wash lettuce, endive, and watercress. Drain and separate into salad-size pieces. Place in salad bowl.

Garlic may be mashed or finely chopped, or juice may be pressed out. Add to greens together with cheese cut into julienne or matchlike strips. Add chili sauce which has been mixed with dressing. Toss mixture lightly to coat greens with dressing.

Serves 6.

RAW VEGETABLE SALAD

3 cups shredded cabbage
2 carrots, grated
1 Bermuda onion, sliced

1 green pepper, julienne
Salt to taste
French dressing (page 215)

Mayonnaise

Wash cabbage. Remove outer leaves and core. Shred remainder. Grate raw carrots.

Slice onion and separate slices into rings.

Wash green pepper. Remove seeds and pith. Shred remainder.

Combine French and mayonnaise dressings until of creamy consistency.

Combine vegetables and dressings. Place in salad bowl.

Serves 6.

HILLTOP ONIONS

2 cups very thinly sliced   2 teaspoons celery seed
  onions   ⅛ teaspoon monosodium
Red-wine vinegar   glutamate
½ cup mayonnaise   Salt to taste

Place thinly sliced onions in a shallow dish. Pour enough
red-wine vinegar over onions to cover them. Cover dish and
chill 3 to 4 hours.

Just before serving, drain onions, reserving vinegar. Mix
onions with mayonnaise and remaining ingredients. Add
2 tablespoons of the onion vinegar.

Serves 8.

HOT SPINACH SLAW

1 pound fresh spinach   2 tablespoons vinegar
2 slices bacon   2 eggs
½ teaspoon dry mustard   Salt and pepper
2 tablespoons sugar   Sautéed freshly crumbed bread

Wash and drain spinach.

Dice and pan-fry bacon until pieces are crisp. Add spinach
to this hot mixture and cook gently until spinach is wilted.
Add mixture of mustard, sugar, and vinegar.

Break raw eggs into mixture. Stir gently until eggs are
slightly thickened. Season.

Put into hot serving dish. Sprinkle top with sautéed bread
crumbs.

NOTE: Any leafy green may be substituted for the fresh
spinach.

Serves 6.

AVOCADO AND GRAPEFRUIT SALAD

> Avocado halves
> Grapefruit sections
> French dressing (page 215)

Wash avocados. Cut in lengthwise halves, giving a slight twist to halves to separate them. Remove and discard large seed.

Peeling of avocado halves is optional.

Lay grapefruit sections, freed from membrane and skin, across the avocados.

Serve very cold with plenty of tart French dressing.

Be sure the dressing is tart. Be sure the salad is served cold.

VARIATION: Orange may be substituted for the grapefruit.

BERMUDA SALAD BOWL

1 head lettuce	½ cup sliced radishes
1 small cauliflower, raw	Watercress
½ Bermuda onion	3 ounces Roquefort cheese

French dressing (page 215)

Separate lettuce leaves. Wash and drain.

Wash cauliflower. Break into flowerets. Slice these into wafer-thin pieces.

Slice onion. Slice radishes.

Place vegetables in salad bowl. Break cheese into bits and sprinkle over surface. Add enough dressing to coat the salad mixture lightly.

Serves 6.

HOT CELERIAC SALAD

4 celeriac roots	1 onion
2 cups water	1 tablespoon flour
1 tablespoon margarine	½ tablespoon vinegar

½ cup water

Wash and cut roots in slices 1/4 inch thick. Cook in water until pieces are tender.

Sauté sliced onion in margarine. Add flour, vinegar, and water. When boiling, add celeriac slices. Serve hot.

Serves 6.

HOT POTATO SALAD

8 medium potatoes
5 slices bacon
1 medium onion
2 tablespoons flour
1/2 cup vinegar

1/2 cup water
2 teaspoons salt
Pepper
1/2 cup diced celery
4 eggs, hard-cooked

Cook potatoes until tender. Drain, peel, and slice.

Dice bacon. Mince onion. Sauté together over low heat until bacon is browned and onion is tender.

Stir in flour. Add the vinegar, water, salt, and pepper and cook until mixture thickens, stirring constantly.

Remove from heat and pour over combined potatoes, celery, and sliced hard-cooked eggs.

Serves 6.

TOMATO CRABMEAT ASPIC

1 cup tomato juice
1 slice onion
1/2 bay leaf
1 stalk sliced celery
1 tablespoon unflavored
   gelatin

1/4 cup cold water
3/4 cup beef bouillon
1 tablespoon lemon juice
Salt and pepper
1/2 pound cooked crabmeat
Stuffed olives

Simmer juice, onion, bay leaf, and celery for 15 minutes. Soften gelatin in cold water.

Strain tomato mixture. Reheat and pour over softened gelatin. Stir until gelatin is dissolved. Add bouillon and lemon juice. Season to taste. Pour into mold filmed with oil. Set aside to chill.

Pick over crabmeat, removing any bony pieces. Slice stuffed olives. Put these into partially congealed tomato mixture. Stir gently.

Chill until firm. Unmold. Serve on lettuce. Dress with mayonnaise.

Serves 6.

TOMATO JELLY RING

2 cups tomato juice
½ bay leaf
2 whole cloves
2 slices onion
Salt and pepper

1 tablespoon unflavored
   gelatin
¼ cup cold water
1 cup diced celery
2 cups shredded cabbage

Salad dressing

Simmer tomato juice, bay leaf, cloves, and onion for 15 minutes. Strain. Season to taste.

Hydrate, or soften, gelatin in cold water. Reheat tomato juice to boiling. Add to gelatin. Stir until gelatin is dissolved.

Pour mixture into lightly fat-filmed ring mold. Set in cold place to congeal.

Prepare celery and cabbage. Dress with whatever dressing is liked.

Unmold ring onto serving platter. Fill center with raw vegetables. Add more dressing if wanted.

Serves 6.

CUCUMBER JELLY

2 cucumbers
2 onions
3 sprigs parsley
1 quart chicken broth

2 tablespoons unflavored
   gelatin
¼ cup cold water
Seasonings to taste

Few drops vegetable coloring

Wash and slice unpeeled cucumbers. Peel and slice onions. Add parsley. Put vegetables in chicken broth. Let them stand for a few hours. Then bring to boiling point and simmer for 15 minutes. Strain.

Soften gelatin in cold water. Bring strained broth to boiling point and add to gelatin. Stir until gelatin is dissolved.

Season. Add green coloring. Do this with a cautious hand, lest the mixture become too green.

Film individual molds, or square pan, with oil. Pour in the gelatin mixture. Chill until well congealed. Serve unmolded salads or squares of mixture on lettuce leaves.

Place mayonnaise on lettuce beside cucumber.

Serves 6.

PERFECTION SALAD

1 tablespoon unflavored gelatin
¼ cup cold water
1 cup boiling water
¼ cup mild vinegar
1 tablespoon lemon juice
¼ cup sugar
½ teaspoon salt
½ cup finely chopped cabbage
1 cup finely cut celery
1 pimiento, cut fine
½ cup grated raw carrot, optional

Soften gelatin in cold water. Add boiling water, vinegar, lemon juice, sugar, and salt.

When mixture begins to stiffen, add remaining ingredients. Pour into molds and chill.

Serves 6.

TOMATO SOUP SALAD

1½ tablespoons gelatin
¼ cup cold water
1 cup condensed tomato soup
½ cup water
1/16 teaspoon onion juice
6 ounces cream cheese
½ cup salad dressing
1 cup chopped celery
¼ cup green pepper
Salt and pepper
Lettuce
French dressing (page 215)

Soften gelatin in 1/4 cup of cold water.

Heat the soup and 1/2 cup water together. Add onion juice and softened gelatin. Stir until the gelatin is dissolved. Cool.

Blend the tomato mixture into the cream cheese.

Add salad dressing, celery, green pepper, and seasonings.

Pour into a large mold, or individual molds. Chill until firm.

Serve on crisp lettuce with French dressing.

Serves 6.

COTTAGE CHEESE RING WITH TOSSED
GARDEN SALAD

2 tablespoons plain gelatin	2 tomatoes, quartered
1/2 cup cold water	1/4 cup chopped cucumber
1 1/2 cups cottage cheese	1/4 cup French dressing
1 cup cream or top milk	(page 215)
2 tablespoons lemon juice	1 cup diced celery
1 teaspoon onion juice	1 onion, chopped
1/2 teaspoon salt	1/2 cup sliced radishes
1/4 teaspoon paprika	1 head lettuce

Soften gelatin in cold water and dissolve it over hot water.

Mix cheese, cream, lemon juice, onion juice, and seasonings and add the gelatin. Stir well.

Pour into a ring mold and chill until firm.

Quarter the tomatoes. Marinate tomatoes and cucumber in French dressing for 15 minutes.

Add the remaining vegetables. Season. Toss lightly.

Unmold the cottage-cheese ring on a large chop plate and place the tossed salad in the center and around the mold.

Serves 6.

MOLDED GREEN SALAD

2 carrots	2 tablespoons gelatin
Celery tops	¼ cup cold water
2 cloves	2 cups chopped cabbage
1 tablespoon salt	1 cup chopped spinach
1 teaspoon sugar	2 grated carrots
1 bay leaf	½ cup minced celery
2½ cups vegetable liquid	2 bunches radishes, sliced

Cook carrots, celery tops, cloves, salt, sugar, and bay leaf in water for 30 to 40 minutes. Strain and discard the vegetables.

Soften gelatin in cold water and add to 2 cups of hot liquid. Mix well. Set aside to cool.

When almost congealed, add the rest of the vegetables. Pour into a mold which has been filmed with salad oil. Chill 5 to 6 hours.

Turn out on platter and garnish as desired.

Serves 6.

COLE SLAW

Cabbage	Seasonings
Dressing	Added vegetables, optional

Chop cabbage, add dressing and seasonings. Add optional vegetables. Note: no set rule for making cole slaw is given. But note the following suggestions:—

Chop, rather than shred the cabbage; flavor is better. Avoid a dressing made with oil. The oil seems to make the slaw slippery. But a cooked dressing, or a hot dressing similar to that used in Spinach Slaw, page 207 may be used. The simplest dressing calls for a little salt, some sugar, vinegar, and sweet or sour cream. Add these separately to the chopped cabbage. Mix well.

Salad Dressings

Salad dressings are used with salads to add richness, zest, and flavor. The dressing may be the exclamation point of the salad.

Dressings lose richness when they are diluted with water left on the salad greens.

Vinegar (either wine, herb-flavored, or plain) and/or lemon juice are used for zest. By the judicious blending of seasonings, the flavor is balanced. Salt, freshly ground pepper, dry mustard, a suspicion of sugar are the seasonings used most frequently. Mashed garlic or grated onion increases the flavor of the salad. Anchovy paste is never a silent partner, but a welcome one with bland greens.

Color may be added by the use of concentrated tomato, pimiento, chopped green peppers, chopped parsley, finely chopped hard-cooked egg.

[214]

But when all is said and done, the two classic salad dressings are the simple French one and sauve, golden mayonnaise.

Many of the commercially prepared dressings are as good as, and frequently better than, homemade ones. Don't hesitate to use them. Most salad dressings contain oil, thus making the problem of rancidity important. Always wipe off the neck of the bottle or jar after taking out the desired amount of dressing. Always cap container tightly. Store opened, but tightly recapped, containers in a cool, dark place.

FRENCH DRESSING

½ teaspoon sugar	¼ teaspoon salt
½ teaspoon dry mustard	5 tablespoons vinegar
1 teaspoon paprika	1 tablespoon lemon juice

1 cup salad oil

Combine all ingredients in a glass jar with a tight-fitting cover.

Shake until thoroughly blended.

Makes 1½ cups.

PIQUANT FRENCH DRESSING

½ clove garlic	½ teaspoon paprika
1 teaspoon salt	¼ teaspoon sugar
¼ teaspoon pepper	½ cup vinegar

1 cup salad oil

Slice garlic thin and add to the salt, pepper, paprika, and sugar. Put in a jar with a tight cover. Add the vinegar and oil and shake well. After 3 hours, remove the garlic.

ROQUEFORT FRENCH DRESSING

1/16 teaspoon Tabasco sauce
½ cup Blue cheese
2 cups French dressing (page 215)

Add Tabasco sauce to French dressing. Crumble ¼ cup cheese into a small amount of dressing and mix well. Add remaining cheese and dressing. Beat well.

Makes 1½ cups.

SEMI-PERMANENT DRESSING *

1 teaspoon gelatin	1 tablespoon sugar
1 tablespoon cold water	Few grains red pepper
2 tablespoons boiling water	1½ teaspoons salt
1 teaspoon dry mustard	1 cup oil
1 teaspoon paprika	¼ cup vinegar

Hydrate the gelatin in cold water. Dissolve it in the boiling water. Cool. The gelatin should be of a thin, jellylike consistency.

Mix dry ingredients thoroughly and add to oil.

Add vinegar slowly and beat vigorously for 5 minutes. Add chilled gelatin. Beat vigorously for 5 minutes.

Allow to stand 10 to 20 minutes. Beat again thoroughly.

WATERCRESS ROQUEFORT DRESSING

½ cup crumbled Roquefort cheese	1 cup mayonnaise
	½ cup cream
¼ cup watercress	

Add the cheese to the mayonnaise, then gradually blend in the cream and beat with a rotary beater. Add the chopped watercress and mix well. This is good on tomato and lettuce salad.

* Reprinted by permission from *Food Preparation Recipes* by A. M. Child and K. B. Niles, published by John Wiley and Sons, Inc.

COLBY DRESSING

½ cup sugar
1½ tablespoons dry mustard
¼ teaspoon paprika
1½ tablespoons salt
1½ tablespoons Worcester-
shire sauce

1 can concentrated tomato
soup
1½ cups oil
¾ cup vinegar
2 tablespoons lemon juice
1 onion, grated

Combine ingredients. Shake well before serving.

COOKED SALAD DRESSING

1 tablespoon sugar
1 teaspoon salt
2 tablespoons flour
½ teaspoon mustard

2 egg yolks
¾ cup milk
¼ cup mild vinegar
2 tablespoons butter

Mix dry ingredients. Add beaten egg yolks. Mix well.

Add milk gradually, then vinegar very slowly. Cook over hot water, stirring until mixture thickens.

Add butter. Strain and cool.

HOT BACON DRESSING

¼ pound bacon, diced
2 tablespoons sugar
1 teaspoon salt
3 tablespoons flour

2 eggs, slightly beaten
½ cup thick sour cream
6 tablespoons vinegar
1½ cups water

Cook diced bacon until little pieces are crisp. Mix sugar, salt, and flour.

Beat eggs and add to sour cream and vinegar.

Put all ingredients with hot bacon dice and fat. Add water. Stir and cook until dressing is thick. Remove from fire.

Pour while hot over greens that have been washed and drained.

CREAMY MUSTARD DRESSING

1 cup 18 per cent cream
1 egg yolk
2 tablespoons dry mustard
¼ cup sugar
1 tablespoon flour

½ teaspoon salt
¼ cup vinegar
2 teaspoons horse-radish
(optional)

Put ¾ cup cream in upper part of double boiler. While it is heating, mix remaining ¼ cup cream with egg yolk.

Mix sugar and mustard thoroughly. Add flour and salt.

Mix dry ingredients with egg yolk and cream. Stir well. Add to heated cream.

Cook, stirring frequently, until mixture has thickened—about 20 minutes. Add vinegar. Beat well. Cool.

NOTE: Horse-radish may be added last if desired.

THOUSAND ISLAND DRESSING

Perfectionists differentiate between Russian dressing and Thousand Island dressing. Actually, the end result desired is a dressing that is highly flavored enough to suit men and to give zest to bland salad greens.

Ingredients which may be added are the following: Chili sauce, sieved hard-cooked egg, minced onion and/or chives, chopped parsley, chopped green and red peppers, capers, chopped pickle, chopped olives.

Use your own discretion as to how many of the above ingredients you add to mayonnaise.

Sauces

THE MAKER of a good sauce is likely to be a good cook, because the same two qualities are necessary; cooking skill and
culinary imagination.

Lumpy sauces show lack of cooking skill. Poorly flavored
ones betray a lack of culinary imagination.

Many sauces have French names because French chefs are
master makers of the smooth, suave, subtly flavored sauce.

Happy marriage of vegetable and sauce calls for considera-
tion of color and flavor harmony. Just because a certain sauce
is suggested for use with a vegetable does not mean, however,
that you cannot experiment with other combinations.

WHITE SAUCE

CREAMY ROUX METHOD: Put fat in heavy frying pan. Set
directly over the fire. When fat is melted, but not browned,

add flour. Stir with a large spoon, scraping the bottom of the pan in so doing. Cook until the mixture is bubbling.

Add one-third of the liquid, stirring surely but smoothly while liquid is being added. Cook until well blended. Add a second third of the liquid. Stir. Add last third. Stir. Cook until the mixture bubbles over entire surface. Remove from fire and season to taste.

BROWNED ROUX: Put the fat in a heavy frying pan, add the flour, stir, and cook until the mixture has changed to a warm tan color.

Add the milk as directed in the preceding recipe. This sauce will not get quite so thick as the first one, since the flour starch has been cooked to the dextrin stage. Dextrin has less thickening power than starch.

HYGIENIC METHOD: Measure milk, reserving one quarter of required amount to stir with the flour. Put remainder of milk in upper part of double boiler. Add flour and liquid paste. Stir frequently until the two are well combined. Cook, with occasional stirring, over hot water for 20 minutes. Add the fat and season to taste.

STANDARD RECIPE FOR WHITE SAUCES

	Butter	Flour	Milk	Salt
Thin	1 T	1 T	1 C	¼ t
Medium	2 T	2 T	1 C	¼ t
Thick	2 T	3 T	1 C	¼ t
Very thick	3 T	4 T	1 C	¼ t

T = tablespoon
C = cup
t = teaspoon

VARIATIONS OF WHITE SAUCE

ALMOND SAUCE: Blanch and chop 1 cup almond nut meats. Brown in the butter. Proceed as for medium white sauce.

CREAM SAUCE: Substitute cream for milk. The amount of butter may be cut slightly. Cream sauce is more creamy yellow than white sauce.

ALLEMANDE SAUCE: Substitute stock, preferably chicken, or liquid in which vegetable has been cooked (for instance asparagus) for the milk just before removing from the fire. When the sauce is cooked, combine a small amount of it with 1 egg yolk. Mix well. Return to the sauce in the pan and cook for 1 minute. Remove from the fire and add 1 teaspoon lemon juice.

CELERY SAUCE: Two cups celery cooked until soft in water to cover, sieved to a purée, may be added to the white sauce. If desired, the water in which the celery has been cooked, or chicken stock, may be substituted for all or part of the milk. One sixteenth teaspoon or less of powdered mace may be added.

CHEESE SAUCE: Select a soft-textured but well-flavored cheese. Cut in small pieces and add ¾ cup to the white sauce. Heat until the cheese has melted. Add paprika. One-half teaspoon dry mustard may be added if desired. Or *see* page 223.

EGG SAUCE I: Two diced hard-cooked eggs may be added to the white sauce.

EGG SAUCE II: Two raw egg yolks may be combined with a little of the hot white sauce, stirred well, put back into the remainder of the sauce, and cooked for a moment.

PIMIENTO SAUCE: Canned pimientoes put through a sieve may be added to the white sauce. The amount of purée required is approximately 2 cups.

PIMIENTO AND GREEN BEAN OR PEA SAUCE: Finely diced cooked green beans, whole cooked green peas, and chopped pimiento may be added in the desired proportions to white sauce.

HORSE-RADISH SAUCE: Add 2 tablespoons finely grated horse-radish, ½ teaspoon sugar, 1 teaspoon vinegar, unless the horse-radish used has been put up in vinegar. Serve hot on boiled fish or boiled tongue.

ONION SAUCE: Cook one slice Spanish or Bermuda onion which has been peeled and finely chopped in the butter for 3 minutes. Proceed with the sauce. Strain before serving.

ITALIAN TOMATO SAUCE

3 tablespoons olive oil *or*
4 tablespoons butter
½ stalk celery, finely chopped
1 small onion, chopped
1 teaspoon root parsley cut fine
1 clove garlic

1 can Italian peeled tomatoes
1 can tomato purée
½ teaspoon salt
½ teaspoon pepper
½ teaspoon fresh basil leaves
½ teaspoon fresh *orégano*
1 bay leaf

Place oil or butter, celery, onion, parsley, and garlic in saucepan and brown lightly. Add tomatoes, tomato purée, salt, and pepper and simmer gently for about 45 minutes. Add the basil leaf, *orégano,* and bay leaf.

Cook for 10 minutes longer.

TOMATO SAUCE

2½ cups tomatoes
1 small onion
4 cloves

2 tablespoons fat
2 tablespoons flour
½ teaspoon salt
¼ teaspoon pepper

Cook tomatoes, sliced onion, and cloves together for 10 minutes. Melt fat. Add flour, salt, and pepper to fat and blend. Add to tomato mixture and cook 2 minutes longer, stirring constantly. Strain.

TOMATO GRAVY

¼ cup sliced onion
2 tablespoons fat
¼ cup dry milk, whole or
  nonfat

2 tablespoons flour
2 cups cooked tomatoes and
  juice
Salt and pepper

Cook onion in fat until very tender.

Mix milk powder and flour thoroughly. Add tomatoes (put through a sieve, if desired), gradually stirring until smooth. Add to cooked onion and cook over low heat, or boiling water, until mixture thickens, stirring constantly. Season with salt and pepper.

Add water to make a thinner sauce, if desired.

MUSHROOM SAUCE

1 pound fresh mushrooms
½ cup sliced onions
¼ cup butter
1 teaspoon seasoning salt
¼ teaspoon white pepper

1 teaspoon salt
2 tablespoons chopped parsley
½ cup sliced green peppers
3 tablespoons flour
1½ cups bouillon stock

2 cups hot milk

Wash mushrooms and peel if necessary. Slice, chop, or leave whole. Sauté onions in butter until translucent. Add seasoning, mushrooms, and green pepper. Sauté mixture lightly. Sprinkle in flour; continue cooking. Add hot stock gradually and stir until thick. Reduce heat and stir in hot milk.

CHEESE SAUCE

½ pound cheese
1/3 cup milk

½ teaspoon Worcestershire
  sauce
⅛ teaspoon mustard

Melt the cheese in top of double boiler. Add the milk gradually, stirring until the sauce is smooth. Add the seasonings.

SAUCE ALMONDINE

¼ pound butter
¼ cup sliced almonds
¼ cup lemon juice

Carefully melt and brown butter. Add sliced almonds and lemon juice.

Serve over asparagus, green beans, or cauliflower. You may substitute coarsely chopped pecans or black walnuts for the almonds.

CHESTNUT SAUCE

2 tablespoons butter	½ cup chicken stock
1 cup boiled chestnuts	Salt
1 tumbler currant jelly	Pepper

Melt the butter. Brown the cooked and peeled chestnuts in the butter. They should break up somewhat at this time.

Add the jelly, chicken stock, and seasonings. When the jelly is melted, the sauce is ready to be served.

This is especially good on chicken fillets, breasts of guinea hen, and baked chicken. When possible, brown the chestnuts in the drippings left in the pan after the meat is cooked.

LOBSTER SAUCE

2½ cups lobster meat	½ teaspoon salt
3 tablespoons butter	¼ teaspoon pepper
2 tablespoons flour	1 teaspoon lemon juice
1 cup cream	2 tablespoons sherry

Melt the butter in a heavy frying pan. Add the flour. When

bubbling, add the cream and seasonings. Cook for 5 minutes. Add the sherry and the lobster cut into small pieces.

SHRIMP SAUCE

Shrimp may be substituted in the above recipe. Use freshly cooked or canned shrimp, being sure that the small black line encircling the outer part of each shrimp is removed. Rinse in cold water and cut shrimp into small pieces.

BROWN SAUCE

2 tablespoons fat
1 slice onion
3 tablespoons flour

1 cup bouillon, meat stock, or water
⅛ teaspoon salt

Pepper

Melt the fat in a heavy frying pan. Add the onion and cook until slightly browned. Remove the onion. Continue cooking the fat until a definite brown color can be seen.

Add the flour. Cook until bubbling. Add the liquid gradually. Bring to the boiling point. Boil 2 minutes. Season. The amount of salt required depends upon the liquid used. Canned consommé is concentrated. If that is used, no salt is required.

ANCHOVY SAUCE

Omit the salt until after 1 tablespoon of anchovy paste has been added to brown sauce (above). Then, if necessary, add salt.

BÉCHAMEL SAUCE

2 cups veal or chicken stock
1 slice onion
2 slices carrot
2 sprigs parsley
1 small piece bay leaf

Dried or fresh celery leaves
6 peppercorns
¼ cup butter
6 tablespoons flour
1 cup milk

Salt and pepper

If concentrated chicken broth is used, dilute to make 2 cups. Many of the canned chicken broths are not concentrated and may be measured and used as taken from the can.

Add the vegetables and peppercorns to the stock. Cook for ½ hour, at which time there should be only 1¼ cups liquid.

Melt butter. Add flour. When bubbling, add the milk and strained stock gradually. Bring to a boil and boil for 2 minutes. Season to taste.

VELOUTÉ SAUCE

2 tablespoons butter	½ cup cream
3 tablespoons flour	Salt
¾ cup chicken or veal stock	Pepper

Melt the butter and add the flour. Cook until bubbling. Add the stock, stirring constantly.

Boil for 2 minutes. Add the cream and season to taste.

DRAWN BUTTER SAUCE

½ cup butter	1 teaspoon lemon juice
4 tablespoons flour	½ teaspoon salt
1¾ cups hot water	⅛ teaspoon pepper

Melt ¼ cup butter. Add flour. When bubbling, add the hot water gradually.

Boil 3 to 5 minutes. Season.

Add the remaining butter in small pieces, stirring after each addition.

SIMPLE CHEESE SAUCE

½ pound Cheddar cheese
1/3 cup milk

Heat the cheese in top of double boiler over hot water until cheese is melted. Add the milk gradually, stirring constantly until the sauce is smooth.

HOLLANDAISE SAUCE

½ cup butter
1½ tablespoons lemon juice
3 egg yolks

4 tablespoons hot water
¼ teaspoon salt
⅛ teaspoon paprika

In making this sauce, be sure there is not so much water in the lower part of the double boiler that the upper part can touch it. The water in the lower part of the boiler should be hot but should never boil.

Melt the butter slowly. Set where it will keep warm. Do the same thing with the lemon juice, in a separate container. Put the egg yolks in the container in which the sauce is to be made. Have this set over the hot water. Beat the egg yolks until they begin to thicken. Add 1 tablespoon hot water. Beat again until they thicken. Repeat until 4 tablespoons of hot water have been used.

Beat in the hot lemon juice. Remove from contact with the steam and beat constantly while slowly adding the melted butter, salt, and paprika. The sauce may be kept hot over hot water. It is best to cover the container.

Beat the sauce lightly when ready to serve.

CURRY SAUCE I

3 tablespoons butter
3 tablespoons flour

1½ teaspoons curry powder
1½ cups milk

Melt the butter in a heavy frying pan. Add the flour, mixed with the curry. When bubbling, add the milk gradually.
Season if desired with salt and pepper.

CURRY SAUCE II

3 tablespoons butter   1 tablespoon curry powder
1 small onion   1½ cups stock
1 tablespoon flour   Salt and pepper

Melt the butter in a saucepan. Add the sliced onion. Cook until lightly browned.

Add the flour and curry. Cook until bubbling. Add the stock and seasoning to taste.

Simmer gently for ½ hour. Strain.

HORSE-RADISH SAUCE

1 ounce grated horse-radish   ⅛ teaspoon dry mustard
1 tablespoon vinegar   ½ cup cream or evaporated
1 teaspoon sugar   milk
                 Salt and pepper

Combine the horse-radish with the vinegar, sugar, and mustard. Stir in the cream or milk gradually. Season to taste.
Serve cold or hot on cold roast meat.

Soufflés

SOUFFLÉ is a word which comes from the French, meaning "puffed up," and this is exactly what this dish does while baking. Basically, a soufflé consists of a thick or very thick white sauce, a chopped or puréed vegetable, egg yolks, seasonings, and stiffly beaten egg whites.

VEGETABLE SOUFFLÉ

(*See* page 220 for white sauce recipe)

COOKED VEGETABLE	* WHITE SAUCE	BEATEN EGG YOLKS
1 cup, chopped	1 cup thick	4 beaten
or	or	4 beaten
1 cup, puréed	1 cup very thick	

† SEASONINGS	EGG WHITES	‡ CREAM OF TARTAR
to taste	4 stiffly beaten	⅛ teaspoon
to taste	4 stiffly beaten	⅛ teaspoon

* Very thick white sauce is needed when a vegetable purée is used.
† Salt, pepper, monosodium glutamate, nutmeg, and celery salt are suggested.
‡ Cream of tartar helps to stiffen egg whites. Its taste is not discernible.

Combine all ingredients except egg whites and blend thoroughly. Beat egg whites until frothy, add cream of tartar. Continue beating until stiff, but not dry. Fold whites into the first mixture.

Pour into a greased baking dish. Set baking dish in a pan of hot water.

Bake 1½ hours in 300-degree oven.

Soufflés baked in a slow oven (300 degrees) will have a rather soft golden crust and will be somewhat dry inside. This type of soufflé will stand for approximately ½ hour if left in a 225-250 degree oven. A browner, crustier, more moist soufflé is produced in a hot oven (375 degrees), but this must be served as soon as it is baked, as it falls very quickly.

Soups

THE MOST famous soup of all times is the one for which Esau sold his birthright. The story goes like this: "And Jacob sod [seethed or boiled] pottage: and Esau came from the field, and he was faint: And Esau said to Jacob, Feed me, I pray thee, with that same red pottage; . . . And Jacob said, Sell me this day thy birthright. . . . and he sold his birthright unto Jacob. Then Jacob gave Esau bread and pottage of lentiles."

In the *Who's Who* of modern soups are bortsch, vichyssoise, and onion soup.

Vegetable soups may or may not have a meat or meat-stock base. The simplest one consists of well-flavored tomato juice, thickened slightly.

Cream soups are rich, smooth, and handsome. Because of their richness, they are better served at lunch than at dinner. In making these soups, a vegetable purée is combined with a rich cream sauce or a chicken-stock sauce.

Chowders are thick, substantial soups using sea food or fish combined with potatoes and salt pork. Some ship-wrecked sailors, so the story goes, found themselves cast ashore with an iron pot (chaudiere) and some potatoes and salt pork. They caught fish and made what we now call "chowder." The most famous sea-food soup, so thick it is a whole course, is bouillabaisse.

"Pease porridge hot, pease porridge cold" is Mother Goose's version of our modern split-pea soup enriched with a ham bone. And "beautiful soup, so rich and green" is Lewis Carroll's description of turtle—either real or mock—soup.

Modern trends in soup making and soup serving are placing emphasis on combining two or more soups, especially the canned varieties. A soup with a totally new and pleasing flavor results.

Smart hostesses use soup-tureen service. The soup, either steaming hot or icy cold, is put into the tureen. This is then placed in front of the hostess. With the soup ladle in hand, she dishes the soup into the bowls, plates, or mugs placed before her. Clear, hot, well-flavored tomato juice may be served with crackers or chips in the living room, on the terrace or porch, or down in the recreation room before the guests are seated for the meal.

VEGETABLE SOUP WITHOUT MEAT STOCK

2 onions, sliced	1 green pepper, sliced
4 tablespoons margarine	4 tomatoes
1 cup chopped cabbage	1 bunch parsley
1 leek, sliced	Thyme, marjoram, savory
3 carrots, cubed	1 tablespoon flour
4 stalks celery, diced	2 tablespoons cold water
3 potatoes, quartered	Salt, pepper
2 parsnips, quartered	Monosodium glutamate

½ teaspoon Kitchen Bouquet

Sauté sliced onion in margarine until onion is light brown. Add vegetables with 2 quarts water. Let the mixture simmer for 1 hour. Add 1/4 teaspoon dried herbs, or 1/2 teaspoon of fresh leaves of herbs. Simmer for 15 minutes.

Thicken with flour stirred in cold water. Let cook for 10 minutes.

Season to taste. Serve hot.

VEGETABLE AND BEEF SOUP

1 pound lean stewing beef
1 beef knucklebone, cracked
8 cups water
1 tablespoon salt
1/8 teaspoon pepper
2 whole cloves
Parsley

2 cups diced carrots
1 cup diced celery
1 cup diced white turnips
2 parsnips
2 to 4 fresh tomatoes
2 cups diced potatoes
3 okra pods

1/2 cup chopped onion

Cover meat and bone with water. Add seasonings, cloves, and parsley and bring slowly to a boil. Reduce heat. Simmer meat for 3 hours. (Do not let water boil vigorously. This toughens the meat.)

About 1 hour before serving, remove parsley. Add diced carrots, celery, turnips, and parsnips. One-half hour before serving, add remaining vegetables.

FRENCH ONION SOUP

18 small onions
1 1/2 tablespoons sugar
4 tablespoons butter or
  margarine

1 1/2 quarts soup stock *
Salt
Pepper
French bread slices

Grated cheese

* Diluted canned consommé may be used; dilute in proportion of one to one.

Peel and slice onions.

Caramelize the sugar in a large, heavy frying pan. Add the margarine and cook the onions until light brown. Keep slices of onion whole.

Add the stock and the seasonings.

Place toasted slices of French bread in the bottoms of pottery bowls. Pour the hot soup over them and dust with grated cheese. Set back in oven for 5 minutes to melt cheese.

POTATO AND RYE BREAD SOUP

6 potatoes	1½ cups sour cream
6 slices rye bread	Salt
6 cups water	Pepper

Pare potatoes and cut into slices.

Add bread, cut into small pieces (leave crusts on bread). Cook in the water until mixture is soft. Put through a sieve.

Add cream and seasonings. Reheat. Serve hot.

NOTE: German rye bread and sour cream unite to make a substantial soup with an unusually good flavor.

MODIFIED BORTSCH

6 cooked beets	2 tablespoons sugar
3 cups stock	4 tablespoons quick-cooking
2 teaspoons salt	tapioca
½ teaspoon pepper	Juice of 1 lemon
	Sour cream

Cook beets. Put through purée sieve. Add stock (chicken broth may be used). Season well.

Thicken with tapioca, cooking until mixture is transparent. Add lemon juice.

Serve in heated soup bowls with a large spoonful of thick sour cream on top.

WATERCRESS SOUP

2 quarts chicken broth
¼ pound lean pork
2 cups watercress

1 egg
Salt
Monosodium glutamate

Heat chicken broth. Add raw pork, cut into thin strips. Boil for 20 minutes.

Wash watercress. Drain. Remove heavy stems. Add to broth. Cook 10 minutes.

Beat egg slightly. Mix with ½ cup hot broth. Pour back into soup.

Season and serve at once.

SPICED TOMATO BOUILLON

2½ cups tomatoes
¼ cup onion
Small bay leaf

½ teaspoon celery seed
½ teaspoon peppercorns
½ teaspoon salt

1 can condensed bouillon

Combine tomatoes, onion, and seasonings. Cook 10 to 15 minutes.

Strain. Add the condensed bouillon. Heat.

Top each serving with a thin slice of lemon.

ST. GERMAINE SOUP

1 head lettuce
1 quart shelled peas
2 cups white stock
2 cups hot milk or cream

1 teaspoon sugar
1 teaspoon salt
Cayenne
2 tablespoons butter

Shred lettuce and add to peas and white stock. Cook until peas are tender. Force through a sieve and return to kettle.

Add hot milk or cream, sugar, salt, dash of cayenne, and little by little the butter.

When boiling begins, the soup is ready to serve.
Serves 6.

Basic Rules for Making Cream Soups

Cook and sieve a vegetable to get a smooth purée. Make a thin cream sauce. Blend the two well. Season to taste, add a distinctive flavoring, or serve with a different sort of soup accompaniment. Do these things and your reputation as a maker of delicious cream soup has been established.

The accompanying table tells you when to substitute vegetable juice or cooking liquid for part of the milk for the white or cream sauce.

The cream sauce may be made in a saucepan or heavy frying pan. But the soup will be smoother and less likely to be scorched or to curdle if the mixing and blending of purée and sauce is done in the upper part of a double boiler.

CREAM BROCCOLI AND CHICKEN SOUP

8 stalks broccoli, frozen
½ cup boiling water
½ teaspoon salt
1 can condensed cream of chicken soup
½ cup broccoli liquid
½ cup cream
Seasonings to taste
¼ teaspoon monosodium glutamate

Cook broccoli in boiling salted water until tender. Drain, saving liquid. Force broccoli through sieve.

Mix 1 can condensed cream of chicken soup, ½ cup liquid,* and ½ cup cream. Add broccoli and seasonings. Heat to simmering. Pour into heated soup bowls or cups. Sprinkle with grated Parmesan cheese.

* Add enough water to the broccoli liquid to make the half cup.

CREAM SOUP TABLE*

SOUP	PURÉE	VEGETABLE JUICE	MILK	FLOUR	FAT**	SALT	ADDITIONAL INGREDIENTS (just a trace)	GARNISH
Asparagus	1 c	½ c	1½ c	2 T	1 T	½ t	Fresh lemon peel	Paprika
Cabbage	1 c		2 c	2 T	2 T	½ t	Carrot, grated	Chopped green pepper
Carrot	1 c		2 c	1 T	1 T	½ t	Parsley	Ripe olive rings
Cauliflower	1 c		2 c	2 T	1 T	½ t	Grated orange peel	Grated yellow cheese
Celery	1 c	1 c	1 c	2 T	2 T	½ t	Celery seed	Minced green celery leaves
Corn	1 c		2 c	1 T	2 T	½ t	Trace of sugar	Minced green pepper
Lettuce	1 c	1 c	1 c	2 T	2 T	½ t	Onion	Sliced candied apricots
Mushroom	1 c	1 c	1 c	2 T	1 T	½ t	Worcestershire sauce	Whipped cream, browned crumbs
Onion	1 c		2 c	2 T	1 T	½ t	Worcestershire sauce	Grated cheese
Pea	1 c		2 c	2 T	1 T	½ t	Mint	Finely chopped mint
Potato	1 c		2 c	1 T	2 T	½ t	Onion	Caraway seeds
Spinach	1 c	½ c	1½ c	2 T	2 T	½ t	Onion	Whipped cream, grated egg yolk
String Bean	1 c		2 c	2 T	2 T	½ t	Onion	Few sprinkles summer savory
Tomato	1 c		2 c	1 T	2 T	½ t	Clove, cinnamon, bay leaf	Minced parsley, minced fresh sweet basil

* c = cup; T = Tablespoon; t = teaspoon

** Additional fat may be added if a richer soup is desired.

VICHYSSOISE CRÉME

6 leek stalks   1 quart chicken stock
3 stalks celery   1 pint cream
¼ pound butter   Salt
½ pound potatoes   Pepper

Wash leeks and cut in small pieces. Wash and cut celery stalks into dice. Cook leeks and celery until soft and light yellow in ⅛ pound butter.

Wash, peel, and cube potatoes. Put with first mixture. Add chicken stock. Cook until potatoes are tender.

Sieve the mixture. Add cream and ⅛ pound butter. Season to taste.

Reheat in upper part of double boiler. Serve hot.

CREAM OF CELERY AND MUSHROOM SOUP

1 cup celery, chopped   2 cups thin cream sauce
¼ cup butter   ¼ teaspoon salt
2 cups fresh mushrooms   ¼ teaspoon monosodium
2 tablespoons parsley   glutamate
2 cups hot stock

Sauté chopped celery in melted butter. Add mushrooms, cut fine. Add 1 tablespoon chopped parsley. Sauté until mushrooms are dark brown in color.

Add soup stock. Bring mixture to boil. Add cream sauce. Stir until smooth. Season to taste.

Serve hot. Garnish each serving with parsley. Sprinkle lightly with paprika.

Vegetable Plates and Platters

"**B**LUE PLATE SPECIALS" served in Ye Olde Tea Shoppe have done much disservice to vegetables. To start with, the background color of the plate is discouraging. But even a plate of another color would be of little help in most cases. Dingy peas, lumpy mashed potatoes, soggy, overcooked cauliflower, and buttered beets that leak red juice onto the limp rag of lettuce under hard-curd cottage cheese can never be saved by the one lone sprig of parsley, or discouraged watercress.

All of which is very sad, because vegetable plates can be pictures, as well as delights of epicure and gourmet.

What is needed?

First, a heated plate onto which will go freshly and properly cooked vegetables.

Second, color harmony and color contrast. The orange yellows of carrots or squash *can* be placed beside red tomatoes or beets in singing harmony if unequal amounts are used. Mashed potatoes, buttered cauliflower, wax beans, and cottage cheese lack color contrast, making an uninteresting and unappetizing dish.

Third, compactly spooned vegetables. A confused mishmash is never attractive.

Fourth, variety in shape and texture of vegetables on the plate. For example, green peas, Brussels sprouts, Lima beans, and kernel corn are much alike in shape. Mashed potatoes, mashed turnips, and mashed squash are similar in texture. Creamed potatoes, creamed corn, and steamed spinach are soft and runny.

Fifth, balance in size. Long spears of asparagus or whole slices of sautéed eggplant are so large they throw a vegetable plate out of balanced arrangement.

The same rules apply to the composition and arrangement of vegetable platters. These may be placed on the buffet table, or set in front of host or hostess. When a vegetable-dinner course is planned, add needed protein in the form of a cheese sauce, or cheese alone, or eggs, poached or hard-cooked or stuffed and sliced.

Flavor accents on a vegetable plate may be salty potato chips, banana scallops, ripe olives, fried apple or tomato slices, pickled peaches or pears, or cucumber pickle fans. These foods give flavor accents and offer color interest and shape variation as well.

Vegetable Platters

Green beans with mushrooms and sour cream, buttered
   onions, tomatoes, celery

Buttered Lima beans, kernel corn, tomatoes, green onions

Brussels sprouts with chestnuts, celery sticks, Zucchini Provençale

Escalloped cabbage, Lima beans, sliced tomatoes

Carrots, Swiss chard, glazed onions, celery sticks

Buttered cauliflowerets, Harvard beets, green beans with mushrooms

Braised celery, peas and sautéed mushrooms, glazed parsnips, potato cakes

Mexican corn, sautéed eggplant, tomato jelly, cottage cheese

Eggplant Italian, celery sticks in green pepper ring, Lima beans

Peas, stuffed celery, coleslaw, buttered beets

Spinach ring, green beans and chestnuts, sliced tomatoes

Butternut squash, kernel corn, broccoli, French fried potatoes

Baked stuffed tomatoes, beet greens, French fried eggplant, sautéed zucchini

Turnip cups with peas, cucumbers in sour cream, buttered asparagus

Vegetable Platters Accompanying Meat

Broiled lamb chops   Currant jelly with chopped mint
Creamed potatoes, butternut squash, raw turnip slices
(cut paper thin)

Roast veal with dressing   Pickled peaches
   Baked sweet potatoes, sautéed zucchini slices, coleslaw

Beef stew   Mustard pickles
Onions, turnips, carrots, potatoes, Sliced Tomatoes 1890 Style

Fillet of beef   Corn relish
   Buttered broccoli, baked tomatoes, mashed potatoes,
            cucumbers in sour cream

Chicken fricassee   Bread and butter pickles
Candied sweet potatoes, corn fritters, buttered green beans

Roast turkey   Cranberry relish
   Cauliflower head with cheese sauce, buttered onions,
             rutabagas

Squab   Currant jelly
   Wild rice, fresh asparagus, buttered zucchini

Roast pork   Hot applesauce
   Swiss chard, candied sweet potatoes, mashed turnips

Planked shad   Philadelphia relish
   Asparagus tips, Duchess potatoes, green beans

Autumn Vegetable Plate

   Place a baked stuffed tomato in the center of the plate.
Arrange yellow sweet potatoes in a sirupy orange glaze, glossy
red Harvard beets, green broccoli, and golden-brown French
fried onions around the baked tomato.

VEGETABLE LOAF

Freshly cooked or leftover vegetables may be used. A good combination is carrots, green peas, Lima beans, and new turnips.

Cook the vegetables separately. Drain (being sure to use the cooking liquid in soup, gravy, chilled vegetable cocktail).

Put a small amount of butter in a frying pan. Sauté each vegetable separately.

Cut the top from a loaf of bread, or from oblong rolls, using as many rolls as there are guests to be served. Remove the center of the loaf, leaving a wall about ½ inch thick (in rolls use less). Butter inside and outside of the bread. Set in a 350-degree oven to toast slightly.

Put a layer of sautéed carrots in the bottom of bread, then green peas, young turnips, cubed, and Lima beans. Sprinkle the juice of a lemon over the top and add a medium-thick white sauce, to which the beaten yolk of an egg has been added after the sauce is cooked. Pour the sauce over the vegetables.

Replace the top of the loaf or rolls and bake for 10 minutes in a 400-degree oven. Serve with the cover of the loaf or rolls left on. Be sure to use the lemon juice and the egg yolk, because it transforms the cream sauce into something as good as Hollandaise. This loaf is recommended highly for service at a party luncheon. Filled rolls lend themselves to buffet service.

How to Freeze Vegetables

Nearly all vegetables can be frozen, but to get good results, choose vegetables that are tender, young, and perfect. Fresh vegetables lose their nutritive elements quickly; therefore, they should be frozen within two hours of harvest. If delay is unavoidable, hold vegetable under refrigeration, but not for more than a few hours.

Vegetables to be frozen should be prepared as you would fix them for the table. Specific directions for preparing various vegetables are given in the chart on pages 246-249.

It is necessary to blanch vegetables before freezing in order to retard the action of enzymes, which bring about undesirable changes in quality and flavor. Blanching may be done in either boiling water or steam. The boiling water method is usually used. Immerse no more than one pound of prepared vegetable in four quarts of water at one time. The water should be boiling rapidly before the vegetables are added. After the vegetables are added, the water should again return to the boiling point (not more than one minute should be required for water to begin boiling again). Blanching time is counted from the time the water returns to the boiling point.

Cool the blanched vegetables in ice water or cold running water immediately.

All packaging material used for storing frozen foods should be moisture- and vapor-proof, to prevent drying out or freezer burn.

Containers should be labeled with the name of the vegetable and the date when it was frozen.

Freezing Chart

VEGETABLES	HOW TO PREPARE		BLANCHING TIME
Asparagus	Wash thoroughly, remove scales on stalks, discard lower white woody portion, and cut remaining stalks to desired size. Sort into groups according to diameter. Avoid iron utensils; they cause discoloration of asparagus.	Small stalks Large stalks	2 minutes 4 minutes
Beans: green and wax	Wash, snip ends, and take off strings if necessary. Break into 1-inch pieces, or slice lengthwise. Avoid iron utensils; they cause discoloration of beans.		2 minutes
Beans: Lima	Shell, wash, and sort beans according to size.	Small beans Large beans Extra-large	1½ minutes 2 minutes 3 minutes
Beets	Cut off tops. If young and tender, these may be frozen as greens. Scrub beets with brush. Scald in boiling water ½ minute. Cool in water quickly for easy packing. Small beets may be frozen whole. Large beets sliced or diced.	Whole beets Sliced or diced	3 to 4 minutes 2 to 3 minutes
Broccoli	Trim off large leaves and woody stems. Wash carefully. Separate heads into pieces not thicker than 1 inch. Split large stems lengthwise. Peel less tender stalks.	Small Medium Large	3 minutes 3½ minutes 4 minutes
Brussels sprouts	Take off loose outer leaves. Wash thoroughly. Discard insect-infected sprouts. Divide into 3 size groups.	Small Medium Large	3 minutes 4 minutes 5 minutes

Cabbage	Discard coarse outer leaves, cut into wedges, separate leaves or shred.	Wedges Leaves Shreds	3–4 minutes 1½ minutes 1½ minutes
Carrots	Remove tops, scrub, and scrape. Cut lengthwise or crosswise, or leave small carrots whole.	Sliced Whole	3 minutes 4½ minutes
Cauliflower	Remove outer green leaves. Break head into pieces not over 1 inch thick.		3 minutes
Corn-on-cob	Husk, remove silk carefully, trim where necessary, wash, and separate into 3 groups, according to diameter.	Small Medium Large	7 minutes 9 minutes 11 minutes
Corn kernels	Follow directions for corn-on-the-cob. After blanching, cut off kernels and pack.		
Eggplant	Wash, peel, and slice into slices ⅓ inch thick. To avoid discoloring, cool in citric-acid solution (3 teaspoons citric-acid crystals to 1 quart water), then wash in cold water. Drain thoroughly.		4 minutes
Greens—beet tops, mustard greens, spinach, Swiss chard, collards, kale	Wash thoroughly. Discard coarse leaves and tough stems. Allow 2 gallons boiling water per pound of greens.		2½ minutes

Freezing Chart—Continued

VEGETABLES	HOW TO PREPARE		BLANCHING TIME
Kohlrabi	Cut off leaves, wash, peel, and dice into ½-inch cubes.		1 minute
Mushrooms	Cut off base of stem. Do not wash or sauté. Package in vapor- and moisture-proof container		
Okra	Wash and carefully cut off stem end. Four quarts boiling water to 1 pound okra.		2–3 minutes
Parsnips	Wash, cut off tops, peel. Slice lengthwise in ¼-inch strips, or slice into ½-inch cubes.	Cubes	1 minute
		Strips	2 minutes
Peas	Shell young, tender peas. Discard any that are hard or too old. Wash and drain quickly.		1 minute
Pepper, green and pimiento	Wash, remove seeds and stems. Cut in halves, slice, or dice.		Blanching not necessary
Pumpkins	Wash, cut into pieces, remove seed and stringy tissue. Peel and cook in small quantity of water, or bake or steam 30–40 minutes. Rub through food press. Cool quickly. Package and freeze. If desired, prepare pumpkin pie mix, following favorite recipe, but omitting eggs and milk. Label carton with size pie to be made and ingredients that need to be added.		

Rhubarb	Cut off leaves, wash stalks, and cut into 1-inch lengths. Blanching is not necessary.	
Rutabagas	Cut off tops, wash thoroughly, and peel. Dice into ½-inch cubes.	1 minute
Squash: Summer	Wash thoroughly with vegetable brush. Cut into ½-inch cubes. Cook as for table use in a minimum amount of water. Omit seasonings. Cool quickly.	
Squash: Winter	Cut into pieces and remove seeds. Steam or bake until tender. Scrape from shell, mash, cool quickly. Package without seasonings.	
Turnips	Cut off tops, wash thoroughly, and pare. Dice into ½-inch cubes.	1 minute
Tomato juice	Put tomatoes in covered pan. Crush slightly to provide enough juice to cover bottom of pan. Heat rapidly to 185° F. (below boiling), cool quickly. Strain. Add 1 teaspoon salt to 1 quart of juice. Package immediately.	

Home Canning of Vegetables

Good vegetables are at their best when served fresh; they rate second best when frozen and third best when canned.

Canning cannot improve the quality of an old, withered vegetable. It takes just as much time to can a poor vegetable as a good one. Therefore it is economically unsound to can anything but fresh vegetables gathered at the peak of their goodness.

Grandmother took pride in her loaded fruit-cellar shelves. But she lived before fresh vegetables were available the greater part of the year and before quick freezing was even heard of. Times have changed; don't feel you must can just because your grandmother did.

Vegetables, with the exception of tomatoes, are practically acid free. Food research has proved that the only safe way of canning vegetables is the pressure canner way where the steam, held within the canner increases the temperature to the point that organisms and their spores or toxic substances are completely destroyed. Even then, homemakers are advised that pressure-canned vegetables, when opened should be boiled for 15 minutes before giving them so much as a taste. The result is safe, but not too appetizing.

If you still think you want to can vegetables, heed the following pieces of advice: Use clean cans in perfect condition (sterilizing is not necessary since stay in canner does that).

If using two-piece lids, always get a new flat piece. If using rubber ring and one-piece lid, always buy new rubber rings.

Prepare and parboil vegetables before putting in cans. Preparation is same as if you were getting the vegetable ready for the table.

Salt may be omitted, but why leave it out unless you have a family on a salt-free diet? Salted vegetables taste better than unsalted ones.

Always have pressure gauge tested in scientific laboratory at the beginning of each canning season.

Read and reread directions that came with your canner. Be sure you know just what to do at all stages of canning. Be sure you do what you know you should do.

Have a kettle of boiling water at hand at all times.

Bring vegetables to boiling point and parboil the required time.

Pour, boiling hot, into prepared jar. Run silver knife blade around inside of jar to break any bubbles or empty spaces. Fill jar to ½ inch from top (exceptions are corn, peas, shelled beans: here you leave 1-inch head space). If liquid in which vegetable was cooked is not sufficient, add boiling water to necessary height.

Wipe off top edge and neck of jar before putting on cap.

Cap each jar as soon as filled. Two-piece lids are completely

Canning Chart *

This table is for use from sea level to 1000 feet above sea level. More pressure is needed at higher altitudes. For each 1000 feet above sea level, add 2 minutes to processing time if time called for is 20 minutes or less. If the processing called for is more than 20 minutes, add 4 minutes for each 1000 feet. When pressure cooker is used at an altitude of 2000 feet or more, the pressure must be increased by 1 pound for each 2000 feet altitude.

		Pressure Cooker		
		Minutes		Pounds
		Pints	Quarts	
Asparagus	Wash, precook 3 minutes. Pack.	25	40	10
Beans (Lima)	Shell, grade, bring to boil. Pack loosely to 1 inch of top of jar.	35	60	10
Beans (string or wax)	Wash, string, cut, or leave whole, precook 5 minutes.	20	25	10
Beets	Wash, leave roots and tops long, precook 15 minutes. Skin. Pack.	25	40	10
Brussels sprouts or cabbage	Remove outer leaves, wash, precook 5 minutes. Pack.	45	55	10
Carrots	Wash, peel, slice or cube. Bring to boil. Pack.	20	25	10
Cauliflower or broccoli	Remove outside leaves, wash, precook 4 minutes. Pack.	25	40	10
Corn (whole grain)	Remove shucks. Cut from cob. Bring to boil. Pack loosely to within 1 inch of top of jar.	55	85	10
Eggplant	Peel, cut in slices or strips, precook 5 minutes. Pack.	40	40	10
Greens (all kinds)	Wash thoroughly. Steam or precook to wilt. Pack loosely.	45	70	10
Hominy	Precook 3 minutes. Pack loosely.	40	40	10
Kohlrabi	Wash, peel, bring to boil. Pack.	45	55	10
Mushrooms	Clean, wash, cut large ones, precook 3 minutes. Pack loosely.	25	35	10
Okra	Wash, precook 1 minute. Pack.	25	40	10

Onions	Peel, wash, precook 5 minutes. Pack.	40	40	10
Parsnips or turnips	Wash, peel, slice or cube. Precook 5 minutes. Pack.	20	25	10
Peas	Shell, grade, use only fresh, tender ones. Bring to boil. Pack loosely to within 1 inch of top of jar.	40	40	10
Peppers (green, sweet)	Wash, remove seed pod, precook 3 minutes. Pack.	35	35	10
Peppers (pimiento)	Place in moderate oven 6 to 8 minutes or 1 to 2 minutes in hot oil or 12 to 15 minutes in boiling water. Peel, stem, cut out seeds, flatten. Pack.	10	10	5
Pumpkin	Cut in pieces. Peel. Steam, boil, or bake till tender. Pack.	60	80	10
Rutabagas	Wash, peel, precook 5 minutes. Pack.	35	35	10
Sauerkraut	Pack, add kraut juice or weak brine.	..	..	..
Spinach	Wash thoroughly. Steam or precook to wilt. Pack loosely.	45	70	10
Squash (Crookneck or Hubbard)	Cut in pieces. Peel. Steam, boil, or bake till tender. Pack.	60	80	10
Squash (Summer or Zucchini)	Cut in uniform pieces. Bring to boil. Pack.	30	40	10
Sweet potatoes (Dry)	Wash, boil, or steam 20 minutes, remove skins. Pack.	65	95	10
Sweet potatoes (Wet)	Wash, boil, or steam 20 minutes, remove skins. Pack. Add liquid.	55	90	10

* Used by permission of Kerr Glass Manufacturing Corporation.

screwed in place. One-piece lid (used with rubber ring) is screwed tightly, then loosened ¼ turn. After canning, this top is tightened at once.

Set jars in pressure canner. Be sure all directions are followed. Process the required time. Let pressure go down slowly. Follow directions for removing jars.

Turn jars upside down for a minute to test security of seal. Immediately return jars to upright position and let them cool in that position.

If liquid has boiled out during processing, the jar is NEVER opened to refill empty space. Letting air in completely destroys the processing you have been doing so carefully.

WATER-BATH CANNER *

Any big, clean vessel will do for a boiling-water-bath canner if it's deep enough to have an inch or two of water over the tops of the jars and a little extra space for boiling . . . if it has a cover . . . and a rack to keep the jars from touching bottom.

The rack may be of wire or wood. Have partitions in rack, if possible, to keep jars from touching one another or falling against the side of the canner.

If a steam-pressure canner is deep enough, you can use that for a water bath. Set the cover in place without fastening it. And be sure to have the pet cock wide open, so that steam escapes and no pressure is built up.

Processing in Boiling-water Bath

For cold pack in glass jars have water in the canner hot but not boiling, to prevent breakage. For all other packs have water boiling.

* Used by permission of Bureau of Human Nutrition and Home Economics, Agricultural Research Administration, United States Department of Agriculture.

Put filled glass jars or tin cans in canner. Add boiling water if needed to bring water an inch or two over tops of containers. Don't pour boiling water directly on glass jars. Put cover on canner.

Count time as soon as water comes to a rolling boil. Then boil gently and steadily for the time given in the directions for the food you are canning. Add boiling water during processing if needed to keep the containers of food covered.

Out of the Canner

Glass jars.—As you take jars from the canner, complete the seals at once if jars do not have self-sealing-type closures.

If liquid has boiled out in canning, seal the jar just as it is. Do not open to put in more liquid.

Tomatoes

Use only perfect, ripe tomatoes. To loosen skins, dip into boiling water for about ½ minute; then dip quickly into cold water. Cut out stem ends and peel tomatoes.

Hot Pack.—Quarter peeled tomatoes. Bring to boil, stirring often. Pack hot in glass jars to ½ inch of top. Add ½ teaspoon salt to pints; 1 teaspoon to quarts. Adjust jar lids. Process in boiling-water bath (212° F.)—

Pint jars..........10 minutes   Quart jars.......10 minutes

As soon as you remove jars from canner, complete seals if closures are not of self-sealing type.

Cold pack.—Leave tomatoes whole or cut in halves or quarters.

In glass jars.—Pack tomatoes to ½ inch of top, pressing gently to fill spaces. Add no water. Add ½ teaspoon salt to pints; 1 teaspoon to quarts. Adjust lids. Process in boiling-water bath (212° F.)—

Pint jars..........35 minutes   Quart jars........45 minutes

As soon as you remove jars from canner, complete seals if closures are not of self-sealing type.

Tomato Juice

Use ripe, juicy tomatoes. Wash, remove stem ends, cut into pieces. Simmer until softened, stirring often. Put through strainer. Add 1 teaspoon salt to each quart juice. Reheat at once just to boiling.

In glass jars.—Pack boiling hot juice to ¼ inch of top. Adjust jar lids. Process in boiling-water bath (212° F.)—

Pint jars..........15 minutes   Quart jars.......15 minutes

As soon as you remove jars from canner, complete seals if closures are not of self-sealing type.

Index